Building Bicycles in the Dark

A Practical Guide To Writing

Building Bicycles in the Dark
A Practical Guide To Writing

John B. Lee

Black Moss Press
2001

Published by Black Moss Press at 2450 Byng Road, 2450 Byng Road, Windsor, Ontario, N8W3E8. Black Moss books are distributed in Canada and the U.S. by Firefly Books, 3680 Victoria Park Ave., Willowdale, Ontario, Canada. All orders should be directed there.

Black Moss would like to acknowledge the support of the Canada Council for the Arts and the Ontario Arts Council for its publishing program.

National Library of Canada Cataloguing in Publication Data
Lee, John B., 1951-
    Building bicycles in the dark : a practical guide to writing

ISBN 0-88753-355-8

    1. Authorship. I. Title.

PN151.L43 2001   808'.02   C2001-901870-3

Table of Contents

Part I
Chasing the Feeling

Part II
Sending Yourself to the School of Yourself
a series of practical exercises in writing

Preface

*T*his book is meant as a very practical guide for the beginning writer and as a means of considering the problems arising for a writer well on the way to becoming a full-fledged author. It should also prove very helpful to the teacher of creative writing who is seeking a clear view as to what it might mean to write creatively. It provides a series of concise essays on how to become a writer, how to write creative fiction, how to write creative non-fiction and how to write poetry. It also gives very practical instructions on how to edit and how to get published. Each chapter in the first half of the book includes a single page of 'dos and don't' on the craft of writing as it relates to the content of the chapter. Building Bicycles in the Dark is full of popular author-tested practical exercises for both creative writer and teacher of creative writing.

Part I

Chasing the Feeling

How to Become a Writer

You do not need anyone's permission to write.
You are born with the permission of the stars.

Serving the long apprenticeship —
the process and the product

In order to talk about the act of writing, it is important to distinguish between the process and the product. By process I mean everything leading up to and culminating in the piece of writing. By product I mean the piece of writing which is the result of the process. Process and product are both inescapably interconnected and at the same time absolutely separate. The former is an action; the latter an artifact. The former is the making of the thing; the latter is the thing being made.

The process is very important because it is in the act of writing that the writer might achieve the greatest satisfaction. The product is often equally important since it exists as an independent and sometimes permanent result of writing. The product is the thing which is made available to the recreator. We've come to know this 'recreator' more commonly as 'the reader'.

All too often, we suffer the misconception that the writer without a reader is not a real writer. And yet the creation can exist as a real thing in the absence of the recreator. A brilliant diary might live a hundred years in a drawer. A beautiful poem can exist in the dark. It need only the light and a willing reader to bring it to life. Think of Anne Frank's diary and the poems of Emily Dickinson. *The Diaries of Anne Frank* had secret pages published only last year; the works of Emily Dickinson though largely unpublished in her own lifetime are now recognized as being among the greatest works of literature.

Of course, the writer is also the first reader. One of the real dangers of being first reader arises from the tendency of the reader to sit in judgment of the work. The reader has the impulse to evaluate and to illuminate. The tendency to evaluate your own work can very easily lead to silencing the inner voice. I call this 'inviting the editor in too early'. The desire to understand one's own work can very easily distract from the doing of the work. We would be far better to simply surrender ourselves to the doing of the thing.

This brings me to the subdividing of the process itself. The act of writing might be thought of as a two part activity. For the most part these two activities should be kept completely separate. The first part of the act of writing involves simply writing. The second part involves reflection and judgment which give rise to editing, polishing and rewriting. This consideration and reconsideration need not result in the changing of a single word.

Chasing the Feeling

Any serious discussion of becoming a writer might begin with the question, 'why write?' And the best answer always begins quite simply—write for writing's sake. Writing is its own reward. Write for the simple pleasure of writing. Because writing is such a pleasant activity, I call the act of writing 'chasing the feeling.' Even now, whenever I write, I am chasing the feeling I feel when the writing is going well. The irony of my predicament arises from the fact that whenever the writing is going well, I am the least conscious of the experience of writing. Athletes sometimes call this experience 'being in the zone.' Whenever the writing is going so well, whenever I am inspired, whenever I am chasing the feeling with such abandon that I can barely keep up, that is when I am least self-conscious and least able to appreciate the act itself. I simply surrender and give in to the impulse as words flood the page. And only in the after-flush am I able to truly appreciate what it is I have been doing.

Even as a very young and aspiring author, I managed to achieve this state. Even before the writing measured up to anything like objective standards of excellence, I was able to chase and catch the thrill which arose from the simple act of giving in to inspiration. I avoided the peril of premature judgment. I silenced the inner editor. I did the writing. I discovered the exhilaration available to those who give themselves unconditional permission to put words on the page, to play at permanent expression, to dream the reader before the reader arrives.

Of course, I hid my earliest work. I did not want to hear I was not Shakespeare. Not yet. I did not want to face the potentially damaging truth which might have silenced the shy muse of the novice writer. My timid muse was as carefree as the wind that blows a random music on the lovely tuneless flute of a bottle mouth. Somewhere deep inside I knew there was much to learn. I knew this instinctively. I knew this as a child on the playground. I knew this as a student in class. I knew it as a reader in awe of great writers. I also knew that if I were to become a writer I needed a patch of time in which to learn my craft without the crabby 'this isn't good enoughness' of my own or anyone else's judgment. If you want to be a writer, do the writing. Chase the feeling. Follow it wherever it leads. Don't write to be admired. Don't write for fame. Don't write to get published. Don't write because you have something to say. Don't write to become immortal. Don't write because you think you know the truth. Don't write because you have an attitude. Don't write to strike a pose in black clothing. Don't write to be cool. Don't write because you like the image of yourself as you see yourself squinting through the heavy burn of smoke motes rising in stage light from Galois cigarettes. Don't write only because you are lonely or because you feel deeply, see clearly, know truly, and are one of those who has paid attention to the world and to the inner life. Write for writing's sake. Write because you write. Becoming a writer begins in the act of writing. Do the writing. All else is peripheral. All else is secondary. Write for the love of words as they appear upon a page. Write for the love of words as they pass your lips. Write for the love of language entering the ear. Write first and foremost for the pure celebration of dictionary music. It has been said that writers are those who have fallen in love with words and the world. And yet, if you would become the best writer that you can be, there is something you must do beyond simply 'chasing the feeling'. The great opportunity which every writer has is the opportunity for lifelong improvement. Unlike athletes who live their life backwards in that they experience their greatest achievement as athletes when they are young and in their prime, a writer's prime might conceivably come at the end of life. The writer's apotheosis might come very late. A writer's glory days might arrive in a last poem, a closing story, a final novel, an ultimate play. I think here of the fictional poet in Tennessee Williams' play, Night of the Iguana. The ailing elderly man of letters therein composes his last poem with the assistance of his daughter, his loyal amanuensis, and then he dies. I think also of Robert Frost at President John F. Kennedy's inauguration, or Canadian poet Earl Birney who wrote some of his most fully realized and deeply moving love poems very near the end of his life.

If you want to become a writer of course, you must do the writing, but you must also do the work. And there is work to do. There is much to learn. Becoming the best writer you can be involves a long apprenticeship. It involves learning the craft so long to learn. If you would be the writer read and admired by an ideal audience of competent highly literate strangers, then you must accept that you have much to learn. You must accept the responsibility of your craft. You must do the work.

Doing the Work

All writing can be broken down into four inter-connected, interdependent components. All writing can be described in terms of content, form, style and presence. The first three can be easily isolated and analyzed. We can learn to decode the code of content, form and style. We can explicate that learning. We can share it with others. We can talk about it and write about it. Presence on the other hand must simply be acknowledged. Or if we write about it, we must catch it in flight as metaphor. It is the inner event. It is the indefinable and irreplaceable thing itself. It is the snowflake of the thing. It is the result of interaction between content, form and style. It is the synthesis which occurs when a highly literate reader brings the mind, the heart, the body, and the spirit to the act of reading. It is the experience itself. It is also something else. It is mystery. It is enigma. It is magic. It is, in the words of Archibald MacLeish, 'wordless as a flight of birds.' It cannot be put into words. It is what poets mean when they say, "poetry is what gets lost in the translation." This is why all creative writing defies paraphrases. This is why all creative writing means not only exactly what it says, but also what it is. In the words of Archibald MacLeish, taken from the much-quoted closing lines of his poem, "Ars poetica," "A poem must not mean/ But be." If you understand Marianne Moore's statement, "poetry involves imaginary gardens with real toads in them," then you will know why I must frustrate the apprentice by also quoting Louis Armstrong who said of jazz, "if you don't know. You don't know." This fourth aspect of all writing is something which must remain available to those who can experience and then express its truth only in metaphor, analogy, and approximation. It can be captured only in the language of evasion and what one might call a higher logic beyond analysis. It cannot be taught, though it can be learned.

This last statement is not true of content form and style. Each of these can be observed and described and therefore shared between readers. And more importantly, there are things we can do as writers to learn how to acquire and discuss these elements of writing by analyzing content, form and style.

First we must have a shared sense of what each amounts to. By content, I mean both the experience which gives rise to the writing and the experience made available to the reader in the writing. The question one might ask of the writing in order to talk about content is quite simple. We need only ask 'what is this about?" If it is a piece of description, then what is it describing? If it is narrative, then what is the story? If it is drama, then what's being said? What is happening? What is the accessible surface of the thing? Most great writing also has deeper waters. But if we begin as writers to look at the surface, then we might better understand those deeper currents of meaning. We might also better plumb those depths by first regarding the surface.

By form I mean mode and genre. By form I mean the inherited conventions and constructions of literature. By form I mean the way in which the writing is shaped and caged. To begin with, by form I mean the four modes of creative writing: descriptive, narrative, poetic and dramatic. And within those modes there are many genres or kinds of writing. Within poetry for instance there is formal verse and free verse. Within formal verse there is the easy rhyme and facile rhythm of doggerel. Within doggerel there exists the nonsense verse, the limerick, the melodramatic. Within verse there is also the more high-minded seriousness of formal verse. Within formal verse there is the sonnet, the villanelle, the Ode...etc.. In order to read and write formal verse there are obvious rules to learn. Within the sonnet, for example, there is the fourteen line structure of the thing. There is the heartbeat of the iambic foot. Etc. More on this later in the chapter on 'Writing Poetry."

By style I mean the diction and syntax of an individual author. Another word for style, as I am using it, is the word "voice." Although all authors of a given language may share a common language such as English, each individual author writes differently. Some of that difference can be accounted for by an author's experience and learning. But most of it may be accounted for by originality and individuality. Great writers are great writers because they write only like themselves. Dylan Thomas writes like Dylan Thomas. Emily Dickinson writes like Emily Dickinson. Even when they throw their voice into the voice of another, still they write only like themselves. We might all console ourselves by saying of ourselves, "I am many voices not my own." And yet, all the voices that we are within our writing arise from the well of one individual. Their truth and beauty arises from the talent and learning of an individual. And that individual might just as easily be us. But we must do the work. We must serve the long apprenticeship. We must learn to pay attention.

It is my firm conviction that the best writing, that is the writing which achieves "presence" arises when content, form and style provide a perfect and integrated relationship one to the other. When content, form and style are complementary, they give rise to the possibility of 'presence' in writing. Only when a poem cannot and must not be a piece of prose, can it achieve presence. Only by experimenting and trying can we learn to listen to the voice within the writing which tells us 'this should be a poem, and this a story, and this a play, and this a novel,

and this a single lyric paragraph, and this a piece of snapshot fiction.'
So how do we learn to listen for that inner voice? How do we learn
about the content of experience which gives rise to content in writing?
How do we learn about form and style? How might we arrive at presence in our own writing?

If you want to be a writer worthy of the attention of an ideal audience of unpaid and highly literate strangers...

If you want to be a writer worthy of the attention of an ideal audience
of unpaid and highly literate strangers, then there is work to do. If you
believe as I do, that we write for the sake of writing, and we share our
work with others in order to honour them, then we have much to learn.
If we would achieve that quality which I call presence, then there is
work to do.

Though the process of writing may be quite different for every individual author, there are elements of learning the craft which are true for
all, though those things may not always be true. I am not concerned
herein with whether the reader of these words agrees with everything I
say. However, I do firmly believe that we must always remain open to
consider what our fellow writers have to say about the craft.

In this world of ours there are things which are always true. There
are also things which are rarely if ever true. There are things which are
never true. And there are things which are usually true. It is this latter
'usual' truth with which I am most concerned. I am hereafter presenting
a prescriptive list of things which I believe to be almost always true. Let
me first give example of what I mean when I say there are things which
are always true.

A fieldstone will not write a poem

Only a very foolish or mischievous person would ever assume the public position that a fieldstone might write a poem. There is the old wag-
gish notion that a thousand monkeys sitting at a thousand typewriters
for a thousand years might accidentally produce the complete works of
William Shakespeare. No one in a serious mood would ever entertain
such a possibility. Fieldstones don't write poems even in the stillness of

of the field. Even the brightest of monkeys cannot imitate the bard. So what? I am writing herein not about those things which are always true, nor about those things which are never true, but rather about those things which are usually true. If you would become the kind of writer who would honour your reader with the best work that is within your capacity to produce, then take heed. Consider the following truths. They go beyond the autobiography of one writer's experience. Each is to a greater of lesser degree a necessary component in learning the craft of writing. Having something to write about includes both living to become a writer and learning the way to put things.

Acknowledging the fact that the following things are 'usually' true invites contradiction. There may arise sincere and successful examples of those authors who come to write quite successfully in defiance of these pieces of common wisdom. I am not attempting to defuse disagreement. I would posit the notion that the exception proves the rule. I would suggest that any writer aspiring to learn the craft would ignore, reject and deny without consideration, at his or her peril. Quarreling overmuch with any of the following misses the point.

For example when an author advises 'write what you know,' they mean when you write about something, or when you write from a certain point of view, you need not begin in knowing, but you had better come to know through research and discovery. I would argue strongly that 'write what you know about' has as an implicit corollary, 'write what you care about' or 'know what you write about' and 'care what you write about.' These two truths are inseparable. Ignorance leads to falsity. Writing arising from ignorance appeals only to those who are equally ignorant.

As a visiting writer I was spending an hour as a guest in a university creative-writing classroom. The students were workshopping their stories. One young author read a brief excerpt from a short fiction in which she wrote about farm animals. It so happens that I grew up on a farm as a fourth generation shepherd. I was my father's herdsman. I had husbanded the cattle, docked the lambs, farrowed the sows. I had spent the first eighteen years of my life among purebred pedigreed livestock. I am the grandson of a much celebrated breeder of Lincoln sheep. I am intimate with the ways of those domestic beasts. This young author read her story which occurred in a rural setting. Her protagonist was a farm girl. Unfortunately, the young author got the world all wrong. In order to write about sheep, she had thought she need only use the word sheep. Her descriptions of the farm girl's experience were an insult to the reader because she had not done the work of learning the world about which she was writing. I told her to go home and learn the weight of testicles. Watch how ram scrotums sweep the dew. Otherwise, don't write about sheep.

When I went to see the popular movie *Babe*, the director lost my willing suspension of disbelief when the farmer gathered up and shipped to market all his farrowing sows. I wanted to stand up in the movie-house darkness, point an accusing finger at the screen and shout "No!" Whoever wrote this piece of cinema doesn't know anything about the raising of pigs. So why would I surrender to this beast fable. I know there are those who would say, 'sit down and just enjoy the movie.' There are those who would say I'm like the dentist who can't watch movies because Hollywood always makes the teeth too white. But then, I would argue, you're missing the point. I want the writer to know everything about everything. Learn the rules and then break them. Fable me fantastical pigs from true pigs. If you don't care about the sky, don't write about the sky. A good reader can always tell.

So, take into account, consider, think about, turn over in your mind each of the following truths and find in it that which is helpful, that which might improve and deepen your own work in your journey along the path to becoming a writer worthy of honouring strangers.

1. **Read.** A writer who does not read will not write work worthy of the attention of strangers. Read for the pure pleasure of reading. Read to observe the craft in others. Read to learn how to do that which is given to you to do. Read poetry to learn how to write poetry. Read poetry to learn how to write prose. Read prose to learn how to write poetry. Read widely. Read everything. Read junk. Read literature. Read cereal boxes and road signs. Read. Read. Read. Read deeply. Read reliably. Read well.

2. **Write.** Write through the junk to arrive at the treasure. Do the writing. Practice you craft. Write. Write. Write.

3. **Learn**. Be interested in everything from the lumber business to the way clocks work. Be alive. Be present. Wake up. Pay attention. Experience deeply. Gather material. Listen to everyone. Hear voices in the wind, voices at the coffee shop, voices in the subway, voices in the absence of voices. Ask yourself questions. Surrender to discovery. Books aren't born in libraries. Learn mathematics. Music. The wheeling of the stars. Look to the horizon and also regard the earth as it is touched by your feet.

4. **Remember everything**. Mine your childhood. Imagine the past. Remember the future. Be in the present. Disappear into the experience. Disappear into the writing.

5. **Acquire the language of your world**. Begin where you live and learn the name of everything. Adam's monomastic task was to name what he found within the boundaries of his garden. We are prisoners of our vocabulary. Acquire words. Be the dog in the bur patch. Gather words as you run.

6. **Fall in love with language.** Celebrate dictionary music. Whether you are singing plain-song or full-song, learn the range of your own voice and be true to the harmonies and discord of your own experience and your own writing. Dare to imitate. Steal. Make other voices your own. You are many voices not your own.

7. **Wake up all five senses.** We live in a culture dominated by the visual. There are a thousand words for colour. We watch television. We watch movies. We listen to the radio. We listen to music. And yet, all great writing engages the entire heart, mind, body and spirit of the reader. Write the perfume of floor wax. Write the taste of the sea. Write the touch of weather. Linger in the cognitive particulars of being human. Learn to bring alive the olfactory language of experience.

8. **Give yourself permission to play**. Pretend. Experiment. Go out on a limb and saw it off. Give yourself the little kick in the head which temporarily skews your view. Clear seeing often begins in blurring. Deep learning is often the result of great confusion. Defy certainty. Make the sort of mud pies children make. And eat them

as children do when they drink tea from empty cups with much pretended sipping.

9. **Learn all the rules of writing, then break them** or use them as you will in the service of your craft. If you think you understand what Picasso meant when he once said, "When I was a child, I could paint like a master. It took me a lifetime to learn to paint like a child," then you know what I mean.

10. **Discover your own taboos, and break them all.** This is not for a moment to suggest that I endorse an immoral code of behaviour. It is based on a personal conviction that there is a clear distinction between liberty and license. The writer must be free to embrace evil and to love the darkest villains. John Milton's most delightful creation in *Paradise Lost* is Lucifer. William Shakespeare's villain Iago is deliciously alive. No one would ever construe that he means us to admire Iago for his evil doing. And yet, it is clear from the writing that Shakespeare loves him. Free yourself to write about that which you forbid yourself to say in polite company. Assume the sophisticated reader. Accept the shame from those who do not understand. To be born a writer means to tell the entire truth and to surrender to the truth in the telling.

Producing the first draft

In the final analysis, it doesn't matter one bit whether the completed work as a published product is the result of white heat and the rush of inspiration, or the result of painstaking and multitudinous rewrites. If the work is good, if it possesses presence, then every aspect of its creation is merely a matter of providing answers to reader curiosity. However, there are aspects of the process which can be learned in order to free the writer from needless obstacles on the path to creating a first draft.

When I am asked how long it takes me to write a poem, my answer is always this: It varies from poem to poem. Some of my best work has simply arrived as if it were a gift from the gods. Some poems simply poured onto the page as if received through inner dictation. I leap out of bed and let the pen chase its own ink. These poems might be said to have taken only a few moments or quarter hours to write. And yet they could not have been written the day before. And they would be gone from my mind tomorrow. I must catch them in flight. Another answer to the question involving those poems is to say, "The poem took only a few minutes, and it also took twenty or thirty or forty years in the making."

There is also another sort of poem. (I speak of poems because I am a poet, but these things also apply to the writing of prose). This poem is the one that arrives as only half-realized and then re-arrives through the process of considering, reconsidering and rewriting. One such poem, "The Art of Walking Backwards" arrived without a satisfactory ending. It took me only a few moments to produce the first draft. It took me two years to arrive at the ending. The wait was worth it. The important thing here is knowing that the first draft was worthy of the wait, and knowing that it wasn't fully realized, and then the final knowing when it was finished. This process amounts to a conscious and competent self-editing. There are ways of achieving the authority and knowledge to edit yourself. I will leave that aside for the time being and focus on the first draft.

Arriving at a first draft, it involves the act of surrender. Do the writing. Let the words flood the page. Chase the feeling. Make a mess. Write in that private half-legible hand that only you can read. Keep up. Approximate the spelling. Guess at the meaning of words. Leave blanks. Move on. Keep going. Let the inertia of the moving hand carry you where it will. Listen to the deep wells of the inner voice. Allow the muse to carry you off. Be the wind. Be the leaf on the wind. Be the tree. Be the earth beneath the tree. Be whatever you need to be to let the writing do the writing. I'm not talking here of stream of consciousness or brainstorming. I'm simply suggesting that you leave aside the second-guessing of an inner editor. If anything about what you are doing makes you fall silent, if it paralyzes the process, if it sets a stone upon your hand, then shun it, silence it, make it go away. Don't judge the first draft even if you're simply writing through the junk. Back up. Start again. Jump the wall. Fill the page. Defy the silence. Make the thing you're making. Play.

Let the piece of writing be what it wants to be. If it wants to rhyme, it will—provided you've learned the art of natural rhyming. If it longs to sing in metered voice, it will—that is provided you've learned to listen to those inner rhythms which give rise to heartbeat in iambic feet or lilting in limerick and other light-versed forms. If it wants to tell a story it will. Let it be a telling voice. Obey the rhythms which arise in the telling. A true poem will be a poem; a narrative voice will emerge in the longer looser rhythms of prose. Practice every form and you'll know when the muse is singing, when telling, when saying, when performing, when stating, when persuading, and so on.

Producing a final draft

Knowing when to let the inner editor into the process is very important. I would suggest that the inner editor might be listened to when the white heat of inspiration dies its first death. That might arrive in the middle of the piece. It might arise whenever you get stuck. It might involve getting up and going for a walk. It might require you to leave and come back. It might require you to stay put and gaze into the silence. Only the experience of writing will teach you what is best to do in the moment.

However, the inner-editor, the first second-guesser of the conscious self might be helpful if we get stuck. Read the piece you're writing. Read it out loud. Go back to the beginning and re-read. Use kinetic energy to overcome the inertia that made your pen stop moving.

The writer and the re-writer

This inner editor is the re-writer. Inviting the inner-editor to consider the completed first draft is a matter of inviting yourself to judgment. It involves improving and perfecting and polishing. One should be able to assume that the proof-reader is there with you. Give a close reading. Check and correct all the questionable spelling. Catch all the typos. Polish the work till it shines.

The equally important and infinitely more difficult work of self-editing involves re-consideration of every aspect of the piece of writing. As already stated this need not result in the changing of a single word. It is certainly possible that the first draft and the final draft might be identical to the last jot and tittle. On the other hand, the writer owes every reader legibility, literacy and authority. If it is in your power to do so, then you should strive to achieve the super legibility which makes the writing available to weak eyes in bad light. If you have the knowledge, then your style should be true to its own best example. Careless errors in grammar, syntax or diction, should not be tolerated by the inner editor. And finally, the last best final draft of the author working alone should have all the authority of being the best you can do by yourself.

When you've exhausted the possibilities of your own inner-editor, when you've arrived at that point where you can no longer be of any help to yourself on your own, then it is time to seek the opinion of someone other than yourself. This is a matter of knowing who to ask and what to require. Friends, loved ones, siblings, relatives, partners, classmates, teachers, anyone willing to read your work and say something about it might be called upon. And yet, friends who love us are often careful of our feelings. Loved ones may not know what to say. Because teachers are taught to care for our feelings, they may behave kindly when there's no real alternative. And the person sitting next to us in class may not have anything helpful to say because they're not reliable as readers, or perhaps they might not be able to articulate that which would prove helpful. If we are fortunate, we might discover ourselves in a friendship which includes adjudication, advice and editing skills. We might find ourselves in a writing group where we are in the midst of a community of mutual mentors. Whatever the case, it is the opinion of strangers which is the most reliable. They need not spare our feelings, because they may never know who we are. If we seek to honour the reader who is the ideal unpaid highly literate stranger, then we need first to consult those who might set us on the path to achieving presence in our work, to achieving that harmony between style, form and content.

Finding a mentor—permission, affirmation, encouragement, guidance and praise

If a writer is seeking a mentor, and if the mentor is to be of any good to the writer, then the relationship must begin in permission and affirmation and move through guidance and acknowledgment. This guidance and acknowledgment involves the mentor listening for the voice in the other in order to hear it when it is true and to make note of when it strays from the voice which is the voice of the work. This involves acknowledging and praising that which is praiseworthy, and noticing and guiding to a solution those moments when the voice strays. This might involve something as particular as pushing the author's nose to the page, or giving a larger advice such as saying, 'dream deeper.' One of the real dangers of a mentor/apprentice relationship is for the apprentice to know how to consider the advice. When to take it. From whom the writer might best learn. If the mentor begins with two assumptions: (1. I could be completely wrong. And 2. The work is the property of the writer and all final decisions are those of the creator of the work.) Then it seems likely that the mentor will be helpful. The writer must also know that seeking someone else's opinion involves taking that opinion into consideration. It does not involve, of necessity, doing what the mentor suggests. Every writer must learn when to hold the ground and when to remove what is precious. Be prepared to take out what doesn't serve the work, however good the writing might be. And yet, be ready to refuse considered changes. Keep what serves the work, even in the face of someone else's authority to tell you otherwise.

The relationship between the apprentice and mentor, and even aspiring author's relationship with the dead authors who inhabit the library with the presence of their work, involves permission first. The mentor gives permission freely by being a writer. The mentor affirms the importance of writing by commitment to craft. The living mentor gives guidance by honoring your work with a serious and well-meaning reading and advice. By listening for the voice within the work. By praising its achievement. By illuminating its effect. By suggesting its moments of failure.

The final product as a published thing...
the feeling of having arrived

As I said at the outset, a writer need not be published in order to call themselves a writer. Do the writing. Learn your craft. Arrive at presence.

If you feel you're ready to publish, ask yourself this: how do I know I'm ready?

One of the ironies of publishing your final draft, arises from the fact that a published work is no longer your property. By publishing it, you invite the stranger into the process. You have surrendered your work in such a way that it might exist in your absence. It becomes the property of the re-creator. You no longer have any real authority over it. You may own it in the sense that the copyright remains in your name or in the name of your publisher. However, by publishing a piece of writing, you have in effect given it away. You have sold it to someone else. I'll say more about publishing in a later chapter. For now, let us leave the product as something in a drawer. A piece of work you can remove and show and which you may carry around with you as you would a photograph. It is an artifact of the process. As long as the page exists and the ink stays true, the product of your efforts is real. You have thereby made something real, the existence of which cannot denied.

The dos and don'ts of how to be a writer

If you want to be a writer...

- Do the writing
- Learn your craft
- Read
- Be a lifelong learner
- Be curious about everything
- Be fully alive and fully awake all the time
- Remember Everything
- Acquire vocabulary
- Learn the rules of writing before you ever dare to break them
- Go in fear of abstractions
- Surrender to the muse
- Give yourself permission to play
- Don't ever give up or listen to anyone who has ever said you should
- Don't take any advice without first considering the possibility that the advice might be completely wrong

Writing Poetry

Poetry is primary. It is pre-literate. We babble before we can say. We sing before we can tell. We utter before we learn to explain. We express with our voices in celebration of pure sound long before we begin to make sense. We are vessels of vocal joy. We cradle unlanguage on the tongue and in the ear. We thrill to private meaning and share that thrill by raising our voice from the crib. We burble in the bassinet amusing ourselves and falling in love with the practice of not making sense. We utter for utterance sake. We express in cacophony and euphony all available sounds. Our themes are sung for ourselves. They're sung for our mothers bending close to listen and hear. They're sung for our fathers throwing us high in the air. They're sung for the dog in the door, the bird in the sky, the bear in the bed and the doll on the floor. There's something we know, something we have to say long before we possess the complexity of language. Our words are random mixtures of consonance and assonance. We possess the formless pitch and tone of needy things. We are body instruments with volume and melody and anti-melody on demand. We bill and coo and wail and cry, unlocking our mouths before we've unlocked the complex code of imperative. We interrogate the world with a riddling tongue right up to the moment we startle the world and ourselves with first meaning. Poetry is also high art. At its best it is the most precious and rare and difficult to achieve of all the literary arts. What begins in dictionary music arrives in the deep, profound, clear-toned and absolutely irreplaceable art of the poem. Change so much as a single syllable and you change everything.

The poem refuses translation. Defies paraphrases. It cannot and must not be spoken of in its own absence lest we return to the poem as source. If we wish to talk of a poem with any authority; if we wish to say what it means, we must return and return and ever return to the thing itself.

Margaret Saunders exquisite imagist poem, untitled and a mere seven words in its entirety, excites five of the five senses.

Through

the autumn mist

a panting jogger

We feel the clammy touch of the chill mist which permeates the poem. We see the barely translucent grey wall of the fog, making us blind to all else in the world of the poem. We hear the 'panting' of a jogger. We taste and smell the ozonated aroma of mist-soaked autumn. And to a very significant degree the entire poem turns on the smallest word. The jogger's identity is rendered uncertain by the use of the tiny and powerful indefinite article 'a'.

And even children might unlock the poem's experience with two very simple questions: What do we see? and How does it make us feel? By see I mean to suggest the entire cognitive experience available to the reader in the seven words of the poem. By feel, I mean reliable emotional and intellectual response to that experience.

Since the only two people present in the mist of the poem are the observer and the jogger, and since the indefinite article establishes with certainty that the jogger is a stranger to the still point of the watcher, then perhaps one of the reliable feelings we feel is unease. Who is the jogger? Might the jogger do us harm? Not likely—and yet, though there's never any real percentage in always expecting guns, we're there with Margaret Saunders' perceiver, wondering. And this experience is all made available in Saunders' seven clear, simple, plain and mostly monosyllabic words. This is the art of poetry. To compress in plain song, and to make available to the mind, body, heart and spirit of a fully engaged and deeply involved reliable reader. And it has been my experience that these mysteries can be unlocked even by very young readers.

An English translation of a Pablo Neruda poem provides another example of how every word counts in the creation and recreation through reading of the experience made available in poetry. The poem in question is another example of the briefest of forms.

> I want to do _to_ you   (emphasis is mine)
> what the springtime does
> _for_ the cherry tree.

The entire experience of the poem turns on two of its prepositions—as in: to you, and: for the. The former preposition has all the imperative of action; the latter contains the implicit generosity of a gift. The former suggests the Eros of the male, the latter of the female. And the poet is both anima and animus, both the lover and the loving, both the action and the result. If you would be a poet, mind your prepositions. Even those tiny words become the metaphor as by this laconic use of to and for Neruda's voice reveals the lover's intentions and his actions and thereby sets free the blessings of spring.

Though poetry is most often thought of as a written art form and we have come to think of poets as writers, in fact it began in the oral tradition. Poetry existed in pre-literate cultures. The earliest mythmakers were poets whose page was memory and whose pen was the human voice.

With the invention of writing, first poets were known as singers. The poet at the centre of Beowulf is called 'singer.' Long before poets wrote and published, they remembered and recited or sang their poems to the accompaniment of the drum or the luthier's instruments. In the ancestry of the dominant western culture, they were minstrels, troubadours, balladeers singing and saying their poems aloud often to the drone of the plucking and strumming of strings. The Biblical shepherd David played the harp beneath his lovely psalms. Thomas the Rhymer was encouraged to 'harp and carp along wi' me.' In the Greek poet Homer we have the Homeric tradition which suggests the accumulation of those two great masterpieces of world literature as a result of generations of remembering and refining what would become the final extant texts, *The Iliad* and *The Odyssey*. If Homer were an individual, then he was also a tribe. Both Ovid and Virgil were court poets employed by the emperor. Their words were written to be spoken for the entertainment of the elite. Even William Shakespeare's great poems for the stage, even those masterful soliloquies which might lay claim to being the apotheosis of English poetry, and indeed human expression itself, even they were written to be spoken and heard. Indeed, we can make and respond to poems as pre-literate beings.

When I was very young, my mother's scolded me for flatulating by saying, "Johnny, who made an odour?" I misheard her euphemism as "who maked a motor?" For days I ran around the house amusing myself with those delicious words. I was celebrating myself in song. I'm sure that was not her intention. What for her had been a gentle disapproving, for me became the sweet refrain and mantra of an incantatory inner engine.

As an adult, looking back on that event, I wrote these words:

Who Maked a Motor?

Mother is humming in the kitchen
like a mosquito under a cupped hand
and I'm her little pre-euphemism boy
my own gases rising
like bread smells
I trail about the house trembling fume.
My mother stops her singing, sniffs,
and politely inquires,
"Johnny, who made an odour?"
Ah, this sweet myselfness.
I am the honeysuckle inside the summer.
It is I who 'maked a motor!'
See how it runs, this splendid fragrance.
How could the world go wrong
in the midst of such perfume?

When my mother said, "Don't be so Persnickety!" that one lovely word became a poem of itself. When grandma said, "cam down!" we cousins amused ourselves for days, weeks, months, years exhorting one another to just 'cam down!' We weren't being deliberately rude. We were simply celebrating the sound by imitating exactly those two entertaining words. We were the little echoes of her heart. We loved our grandmother and said so over and over again in that refrain, "cam down! cam down! cam down!"

Even a complex poem might result from the accident of a child's free voice. When poet John Tyndall was talking to his young son about tornadoes, his son said to him, "Daddy, I want to find the bones of a tornado." John knew instantly this line was the gift of a poem being freely given. This child's logic unlocked a way of seeing and saying which our adult learning had rendered temporarily unavailable. Of course tornadoes are simply destructive forces of nature. But 'the bones of a tornado' gave rise to the possible archeology of storm. John went away and wrote what became one of his best poems, the germ of which was this child's longing expressed beautifully in that line— "Daddy, I want to find the bones of a tornado." John was listening. Poets must listen. The air is sometimes thick with the accident of lyric.

When my elder son Dylan was barely five, he came to me and said he had written a poem. This poem he'd composed was created before he even knew his a b c's. He came to me with the poem in his head. He recited these words to me on the beach one summer in Turkey point before he knew how to read and write.

> *Clouds in the sky.*
> *Trees in the forest.*
> *Wolves in the forest, also.*
> *And me in my house.*

I have remembered and cherished those lovely words ever since I first heard them. It was the first, last and only poem he ever brought me. When I asked him for a title to his poem, he made up some long forgotten non sequitur just to please me, just to satisfy my adult sense that a poet must consider the need to give his poem a title. But he was clearly finished with those four lovely lines. He even intuitively understood how to perform the poem by breathing the punctuation and spaces. He knew how to pause and recite the pauses so I might transcribe his intention and encode the line breaks and honour the ghost of white spaces. He had indeed composed a poem. He had made words sing. It only wanted the memory of a good listener and the action of a meticulous amanuensis to capture the event of that poem in flight.

This little poem of my son's has the artlessness of great art. Though it is not a great poem, it is certainly better than bad. It sings just enough to be lovely. Its depths are easily plumbed. It is rooted and simple and true. Within those four lines the universe of the child is unfolding as it should.

So how might we learn to listen when the voice is great within us? How might we train ourselves to capture in language the song of ourselves as a poem? For although as I've said at the outset, 'poetry is primary, pre-literate, oral, and available to children even before they can speak or comprehend,' on the other hand, great poetry, great art is the result of much learning and practice of craft. Recently I was reading a novel in which one character criticizes an aspiring artist's work by saying, "there's not enough artifice to make it art." And of course all art is a human creation and therefore contains an essential degree of artifice. Too much artifice and it becomes artificial; too little and it is bland. Too little artifice and we invite the wrath of the reader who in the words of Truman Capote might bark, "that's not writing; that's typing!" Art without artifice is not art at all. Art without artifice is bland as thin water. Art with an excess of artifice is fever in the food. The former is underwrought; the latter overwrought.

Poetry like all art seeks a balance between natural voice and learned voice. In order to write poetry, we must also learn to write poetry. In order to learn to write poetry we must set the learned voice free.

What is poetry? Is poetry a dog?

Defining poetry in the absence of the poem is like suggesting we might conjure the thing being named in the naming. To a large degree, asking the question presupposes experience and comprehension. If you want to know what poetry is—go read a thousand poems and then ask. But how might we know we're reading poetry, when perhaps we don't yet know what poetry is. And so we circle and circle in circles circling back on themselves. And yet, we know a poem when we read one. It lifts the hair on the nape of the neck with the pleasure to be had in the reading. We also might know a 'not-a-poem' when we read that. Of course there are those who would acknowledge only for the most formal and high-minded of work and they would quarrel with the freer spirits of the any-thing-goes anti-elitists. That gets us nowhere. There's room in the read-ership for anything that gives pleasure in re-creation. The mischievous Marshall McLuan said, 'art is anything you can get away with.' Okay, but if that is so, then art is a great con. I'm not willing to concede that. For me the greatest pleasure in creating a poem arises out of the inter-action between learning and freedom. The wild energy and originality of the human voice in flight caged in the beautiful artifice of form and convention results in the best of poetry.

Any discussion arising from the question, 'what is poetry?' involves the irony that if you don't know the answer to begin with, then you're simply involving yourself in an exchange of ignorance. And yet even very young children know a poem when they've read one. So perhaps we arrive at wrestling with the question in any meaningful way only after we know the answer by reading poems and poems and more poems. If we don't know what we mean when we ask the question, we might give ourselves what I call *a little kick in the head* which skews our view enough to get us started. My question is this: is poetry a dog? Even a child knows that a dog is not a poem. A dog is a kind of animal. A sort of furry, four-legged, tail-wagging mammal we might keep as a pet. Bark! Bark! So too, we might begin answering the question, 'what is poetry?' If a dog is a kind of animal, then poetry is a kind of some-thing. If a dog has characteristics, so too must poetry possess charac-teristics and so on.

Following this dog-defining philology we might arrive at a defini-tion of poetry which satisfies our question, "what is poetry?"

Poetry is a kind of writing wherein the poet uses imagination, mem-ory, experience, feelings, dreams, desires, etc. to create a poem. Poetry sometimes rhymes and employs a regular rhythm or meter. Poetry is often written in lines and stanzas. To quote a child, "poetry is when words sing."

If poetry is a kind of writing, then what of pre-literate poetry and what of the oral tradition? If poetry rhymes or employs meter, then what of free verse? If poetry is arranged in lines and stanzas, then what of concrete poetry, sound poetry, performance poetry, the tone poem, the prose poem and so on? You see the problem.

Definitions, though helpful and sometimes clarifying to those who already know the nature of poetry, are also reductive and either overly exclusive and needlessly elitist, or so general and generic as to be meaningless. And yet, we know when a poem is a poem, and we know when it is simply something else pretending to be something it isn't.

Perhaps the major problem with attempting to define poetry so that we might know we are writing poetry when we're writing it, arises from the paradox of definition. We can only understand and experience the thing being defined when we've read and read and read. Definitions are the result of knowing not the source of knowing. They are both the end point of experience and the shared understanding of experience and the starting point. If you want to arrive at a clear and reliable answer to the question, 'what is poetry?'—then there is no substitute for reading. If you want to write poetry, then read poetry, imitate exemplars, find your voice through practicing your craft and reading the masters of the art. And if you would write great poetry, with a clear eye, an engaged mind, a trained sensibility, then read great poetry. You will find then that deep waters need not be muddy, and shallow waters though muddied by deliberate obscurity of the amateur, merely seem deep because they are murk.

1. **See all the do's and don'ts of *how to become a writer*...**they also apply to the writing of poetry.

2. **Read every kind of poetry and practice** the craft of writing poetry by imitation. Conceive of the poem as a visual object. Conceive of it as a thing to be performed. Conceive of it as something read in silence and solitude. Shape the language and grapple with the

twin concerns of freedom of expression and the cage of form. Read William Blake's poem, "The Tiger" and think about Blake's phrase, "fearful symmetry." Ask of this the most widely anthologized poem in the entire English cannon, what is the balance between creative energy and the requirements of art.

3. **Write the poem as heightened utterance,** a performance piece as brave as a shout or shy as a whisper with the voice set free or caged.

4. **Write the poem as light verse,** engage the shallow themes which entertain the child within us. Explore, experiment, and learn the rigors of rhyme. Discover the natural voice within easy rhyme and facile rhythms of allsense, nonsense, and the hyperbolic tongue twists of doggerel as art. Dare to play with lilt and limerick. Internalize the rhythm of words. Listen with the inner ear.

5. **Write the poem as formal verse.** Master the heartbeat of the iambic foot which is central to the early sonnet. Learn and practice the rigors of lyric and narrative forms. Learn to write an ode, a sonnet, a villanelle. Learn the laconic compressions of plain song and the baroque rhetorical flights of the likes of Dylan Thomas and Gerard Manley Hopkins.

   Ask yourself of every poem you read—what is this thing? How was it made? What is it about? How is it about what it is about? And dare to accept the mystery beyond understanding, the magic beyond what you can share with another.

   Dare to echo and imitate everyone within your attention from the easy and silly entertainments of Edward Lear and Lewis Carrol to the metaphysical and difficult poetry of T.S. Eliot. Find your own voice through the voice of others.

6. **Read free verse as it is practiced by the best practitioners.** Observe their art closely. Notice that in the best of them, that free verse, though free from the conventions of formal verse, is not truly free at all. The best free verse in fact is not simply prose broken into lines and stanzas.

   Rather, free verse obeys the very same singing, telling, saying voices of formal verse in the absence of the artifice of meter and end-line rhyme. The free verse lyric is 'new song' not 'no song."

This knowledge of free verse arises only as a reliable reader response to lyrical and formal engagements of the author. One of the most frequently misunderstood and badly taught modern poets is the highly formal poet, e.e. cummings. Much can be learned by a close reading of his poems. cummings is one of the great early American masters of the free verse form. On first glance, his poems appear to be free from artifice. Yet his voice has all the authority of craftsmanship and care of more obviously formal verse. Though his rhythms do not often adhere to the meter of formal verse, one only need consider a few of his poems to recognize the poet as someone raising his lyrical voice in celebration and song.

Consider these first lines of three of his poems:

> *my sweet old etcetera*
> *when faces called flowers float out of the ground*
> *all ignorance toboggans into know*

Or if one considers the apparent randomness of his punctuation, as in the poem "Chansons Innocentes" one soon comes to the realization that there is a very tight and highly controlled connection between technique and meaning; between artifice and affect.

Letting the Editor in—first to last draft

Know this! The writing of a poem begins alone. It is performed in solitude and it involves a deep communion with the self. At its best the process of producing a first draft involves catching the poem in flight. We rush to keep up with the pen. If we struggle, we struggle to set the thing free.

When the first draft seems finished, we begin the second guessing. We may need to set the poem aside for a while. We might simply honour the first draft by making a polished proof-read version in our own best hand, or better yet, on a typewriter or computer print out. Then when we are ready to see the poem objectively, we might begin the process of considering and re-considering the poem in an effort to achieve the poem as our own best work. This involves reading and re-

reading the poem and listening for when we've strayed from the 'inner voice' of the poem. When we're on the verge of ruin, then we must seek another reliable and helpful opinion. This first audience to the poem in progress might be a partner. It might be a friend. It might be the fellow members of a poetry group. It might be an audience of strangers at the poem's first public reading. We must be prepared to listen and consider all opinions with special attention to those whose suggestions honour the poem. We need not heed every piece of advice. Never change a poem simply because someone says you should.

In order to know the best final draft of the poem, we must practice both the craft of writing and the art of rewriting. This involves knowing what works and finding those suggestions which are helpful. This too can be learned only in practice.

The Dos and Don'ts of Writing Poetry

Do:

- give yourself permission to write what you write
- set your voice free but be particular...the quality is in the details
- learn your craft by reading poems
- find your voice through imitation and practice
- surrender to the poem...listen for its voice...its voice is within you
- sing rather than state
- 'image' rather than say
- engage all five senses
- be careful in your line breaks, let them serve the poem...a poem is not simply prose broken up
- rhyme well, rhyme naturally, rhyme in service of meaning
- internalize the rhythm of the poem
- ...meter which is a frequent companion of rhyme requires consistency...don't cheat
- re-write everything...even if you leave everything exactly the same

as in the first draft, at the very least you must consider and reconsider everything you write and be prepared to sacrifice the very best lines in the name of what is best for the final poem

Remember, even bad poetry is sincere, so:

- don't employ deliberate obscurity, it is a vice of much bad poetry
- don't ever confuse carelessness with freedom...they are not the same thing
- don't ever use polysyllabic mouthfuls... a poem is not a scholarly paper and you're not showing off your learning
- don't ever rhyme simply for its own sake, if a poem wants to rhyme it will...incompetent rhymes are those rhymes in which we allow the rhyme to tyrannize over the meaning...rhymes which force us to say things which destroy that which is best in the poem are 'bad' rhymes
- don't break with the forms and conventions until you've learned them well

Do find the balance between inspiration and the well-trained imagination.

Writing Fiction:
Lying to Tell the Truth

When I was a teacher of secondary school English asking my students "what is fiction?' there would always be someone willing and anxious to tell me, "Fiction is lying." And of course to a degree, that is accurate. Fiction involves invention in the telling of stories which are in one sense untrue. And yet, if fiction is lying, then it might be more accurate and helpful to state that fiction is lying to tell the truth.

Though my own paternal grandfather was an avid reader, he had little or no patience for fiction. To him it was a waste of time because for him fiction involved a falsity unworthy of his attention. In a letter written to his niece near the end of his life, he stated his distaste and distrust of fiction with these words: "I hardly ever read fiction. I like facts, not illusion." And yet he loved the debate arising from a close reading of the Bible. He wrote pages of correspondence in response to the mythologies of his Irish ancestors. He sought meaning in the creation myths of many cultures. And thus in contradiction to his contention that fiction is 'illusion', he revealed the sensibility of a lover of fiction. He suffered the common misconception that the truth is made available simply through an accumulation of facts. If the court of his mind required the facts, then one might set those facts and their stingy small truths against what Canadian novelist Margaret Laurence has to say about fiction and fact. In her great master work, *The Diviners*, her fictional protagonist, Morag Gunn, is a writer of fiction. In that novel Morag writes of herself and her fiction— "...A daft profession. Wordsmith. Liar, more likely. Weaving fabrications. Yet, with typical ambiguity, convinced that fiction was more true than fact. Or that fact was in fact fiction."

Fiction is writing drawn from the imagination. Non-fiction is writing drawn from memory, history and fact. In a narrow sense, the word fiction relates only to the subject matter and content of writing. However, as it is with all creative writing, questions concerning the work of the imagination might be divided into concerns of content, form and style.

Content in fiction—what stories are mine to tell?

What stories are mine to tell? How might I find them? How might I unlock my own fictional story chest? These questions amount to the 'may I' and 'can I' of fiction writers. "May I tell you a story?" and, "Can I tell you a story?" are very different questions. The former involves permission. The latter involves discovery and learning. The former is easy to answer. The latter requires more consideration and of course as always requires the learning of craft. Let us begin by considering the former. May I tell you a story? You need no one's permission but your own. You must simply do the telling. You must do the writing. However, if you require an audience, if you request and require a reader's attention, then you must honour your reader by telling a worthy story well.

Where do the stories you have to tell come from? What stories are given you to tell? How might you unlock your own inner life? How might you excite your own imagination and thereby discover what it is you have to say? What is your material? The answer to each of these questions will in part lead to an answer of the more complex question, "how do I tell the stories it is given me to tell?"

If you have paid attention to life and if you have a good memory, then you have within you the first source of story. The material for fiction begins in your own life. Be prepared to mine your childhood. Begin with the conviction that your own life is interesting and worthy. First fictions often begin in simple semi-autobiographical tales. The imagination is fired and informed by childhood. Much early fiction begins in who we are and where we live and what has happened to us thus far in our lives. We might learn to unlock those tales within us by mining our own past. The great Canadian semi-autobiographical novel, *Who Has Seen the Wind,* is in one way a fictionalization of W.O. Mitchell's prairie childhood. In part, it is a novel arising from two very simple questions: 'What if a boy grew up on the prairies?' and 'what if that boy's beloved father died before his son came of age?' Let us not trivialize Mitchell's achievement by diminishing it, but rather let us begin with the simple acknowledgment that the story begins as an answer to these two aforementioned questions.

Dragging a tree through your life

In a way, all fiction can be said to begin as "what ifs." In order to unlock the what ifs of our own private past, we might take example from the concept of dragging a tree through our lives. Since my own culture and geography includes the presence of trees I choose this common object as an example. Begin with the generic word tree. Move through the general to the more particular. For example the word tree leads to the words coniferous and deciduous. The latter word leads us to maple, birch, beach, linden, larch, poplar, ash, basswood, oak, elm, walnut, willow and so on. Then remember and consider a particular elm, a childhood oak, a family willow. Thus by moving backwards from the general through the particular, you might excite a poignant private memory which might become the source of story.

When I first used this exercise at the University of Maine, the results were amazing and very moving. The word tree is dull and generic. The words elm and maple and larch, though lovely are in and of themselves merely decorative. When the writers in the class began to move into their own private tree of memory, they were able to tell stories which made us laugh and cry. We became involved in remembering, sharing and honouring one another's memories with our attention.

One young woman remembered a catalpa tree. As an innocent young woman of around fourteen, she had lain down beneath that tree and pretended she was a young farrowing sow and nursed her siblings.

To her it was a strangely innocent tale. It reminded her of her love for her siblings. It reminded her of her connection to the animal world. And although it contains the possibility of titillation, it was told so well that it was almost devoid of erotica.

A man remembered climbing a white pine and sitting in the crotch of a strong branch and weeping because his wife had left him. A third writer remembered the welts left on her flesh when her mother switched her with willow catkins for having been disobedient. A writer who grew up on a farm remembered a killing tree where they used to slaughter the hogs and hang them to let their screams go dry on the wind. Another recalled a swing maple from which his grandfather had hung a rope swing. Another remembered an apple tree he'd climbed as a boy with his friends to satiate his appetite on green apples. And so on. These were but the beginnings of story. But these beginnings were rooted in the particulars of childhood. They were moving or funny because they were so rooted. Of course sincerity of feeling is never enough to make a story compelling. The quality of the telling is also a necessary component.

If memory is one source of story, and experience another, then imagination and invention are also the source of story. We might unlock the imagination, and see its diversity through the generation of 'what ifs.' Of course all stories worthy of fiction contain conflict and crisis. But all stories begin with these simple what ifs. And these what ifs of our own stories and story inclinations might be best organized according to genre, so that we might explore the nature of our own particular impulses.

These what ifs give rise to the beginnings of plot. They ask and answer the question—what is the story I am setting out to tell? They are merely the catalyst provoking the imagination. They simply generate a story idea. The next decision we make once we've gotten the germ of an idea involves deciding who it is that gets to tell the story we've been given to tell. Whose voice will we use? Alistair MacLeod poses the question this way, "Who will be the voice to carry this forth?" And as we are many voices not our own, this is a very important first decision. Who will tell the story also suggests "who would know the story?" Does it require first person narration? Is it of necessity a tale to be told by third person omniscient? The answer to these questions is arrived at only through practice of craft and allowing the voice to become real in the telling. This leads us from considerations of content to considerations of style.

Voice and Style:
Finding your own best voice for the telling

In deciding who gets to tell the story, the author must not only choose the teller, but also decide upon the teller's point of view as observer and participant in the tale. The author must be true to the attitude of the teller and the teller's voice. The voice of the narrator is most affecting and successful when it arises from the best impulses of the story being told. The content of the story and the identity, perceptions, and attitudes inherent in the voice of the teller are ineluctably interconnected. A story might succeed or fail to engage the reader based upon the author's choice of narrative voice and the author's ability to sustain that voice throughout the tale.

Fiction is most often written in prose. Prose writing in fiction involves the organizing of words into sentences and paragraphs. Becoming a master of prose writing in English involves the mastery of standard written English. Though it may be said of English, that it is not just one language, but many, it is also true that if a writer would use language well, gracefully, powerfully, and effectively, then surely an author must learn to use language correctly. All dialects, all variations on English return to the well of proper English which has the authority of tradition and agreed upon meaning and usage. The context of culture and subculture requires a knowledge of this tradition and this central agreed upon standard. One can tell a moving story well and effectively in any engaging and consistent voice, but we must also learn the grammar, syntax, spelling and punctuation of our shared culture. And within the one voice of prose, there are four available modes. They are descriptive, narrative, dramatic, and expository. Writers might use them all to varying degrees in the writing of fiction.

Both the choice of narrator and the nature of the story being told have an influence on the mode of the telling.

Description: the descriptive voice

The descriptive voice in prose fiction is directly related to the movement of time. In description, the writer is freezing the moment. Much like a photograph, the author is stilling the moment and providing the reader with an image. However, unlike a photograph which is purely visual, writing must excite all five senses. If an author would make the still moment worthy of the reader's attention, then the writer must make the moment real. Even in the most imaginary of settings and circumstance, effective description requires the engagement of the entire cognitive experience. In the best descriptions, we see, hear, taste, smell, and touch the experience.

Consider these descriptive sentences taken from a piece called, "The Boy With the Duck on His Head," "The boy is running, his mad hands flashing like a feather plucker in the belly down, the duck cleated so the toe webs are stretched open and rubbery, adhering to the flesh below the hair. The boy is running for the farmhouse where his grandfather is at the gate jacking the manure from his boots, first one, then the other, so the sheep dung is there on the jack blade whickered with straw, and dark green, lincoln green, cud green, apple-shit green, a high sweet rose-garden stink instant and to be relished." Notice the toe webs are 'rubbery'. Note the litany of greens, the tactile use of the word whickered, the olfactory use of "high sweet rose-garden stink..." and the celebratory use of the word "relished."

Another example of five-senses description might be observed in the opening paragraph of *Stella's Journey.*

> More than forty years a ghost. I've faded now, the very sub-
> stance of my specter gone like snow landed on warm ground.
> But I too was born once. Born at home, like most. While the
> small mad calliope of the kitchen kettle shrilled on the iron
> stove, I came caterwauling into the world on a fine day, the
> ninth of June, 1885. My mother fair, though temporarily
> occupied; my father handsome and well-healed, handing out
> cigars. I flopped into the doctor's hands like greased dough.
> Cut loose, I sucked at life. The warm milk of mother Mara in
> my mouth sweet. I would live seventy years. I would die in

bed in a city some fifty miles from home. My husband's words for that passing, "Is she gone then?" Surely my life had purpose. Consider then my hours on earth and the great darkness before and after.

My name, Stella, means star. I rose in that ancient heaven and shone for twenty-some thousand days until the autumn solstice fell on the farmhouse, and I twinkled out like a sinking spark.

Consider also Hemingway's opening paragraph to his novel, *To Have and Have No*t. Note the absence of adjectives.

You know how it is there early in the morning in Havana with the bums still asleep against the walls of the buildings; before even the ice wagons come by with ice for the bars? Well, we came across the square from the dock to the Pearl of San Francisco Cafe to get coffee and there was only one beggar awake in the square and he was getting a drink out of the fountain. But when we got inside the cafe and sat down, there were the three of them waiting for us.

Narration—the telling voice

The narrative mode is the telling mode. If description freezes time and is photographic, then narration follows the rhythms of time and is filmic. That is not to say that narration is of necessity obedient to chronology. Narration might in fact leap back and forward from present to past to future. It might leap over time in either direction. Narration does involve the passage of time and since the narrative voice is the telling voice, it is the voice through which the narrator relates event. The narrative voice tells us what is happening over the passage of time.

Dramatic Mode—Dialogue and the saying voice

The dramatic voice in fiction is the saying voice. It is the voice of dialogue. Unlike the narrative voice which follows the larger rhythms and patterns of time past, time present, and time future, the dramatic voice or the saying voice, the voice of dialogue can be said to be true to real time. Within the context of the story, people say what they have to say in exactly the amount of time it takes to say it. Of course a reader might accelerate the saying by reading quickly, but in the imaginary context of conversation on the page, the reader acknowledges the true chronology of what is being said.

In some ways, dialogue is the most difficult to write. A piece of description might get away with being flat or overly lyrical. Narration might plod or race or stumble or become briefly dull. But when a character speaks, the reader listens and easily hears when the voice goes wrong.

Often the masters of dialogue from whom writers can learn the most about writing dialogue are writing popular fiction. Often authors of popular fiction have paid closer attention to the way people talk.

One of the great failures of the much-admired author, Robertson Davies, is his use of dialogue in his masterpiece, *Fifth Business*. It is small criticism, but nonetheless true to accuse his learnèd characters of speaking with one voice and his minor, small-town folk of speaking in the misheard caricature of the bumpkin. These are the two extremes of the snob. Country people don't talk like that. They simply aren't that dumb. And most educated people don't talk like his educated people. They're generally not that smart.

If one would write dialogue, then one should listen well and be true to what one hears. The best dialogue serves both the character and the story.

Exposition—the informing voice

The expository voice in fiction is the most formal. It is the voice whereby the author gives the reader necessary information. It is the least natural of the four modes of prose writing in fiction. If it is necessary to inform the reader, an author might be well advised to seek a way of blending the information into the narrative. However, this is not always possible. In order to avoid expository globs which interrupt the flow of the story, expository writing in fiction should be integrated and incidental. Barbara Kingsolver's novel, *Prodigal Summer*, provides a brilliant example of sending the reader to school.

One of her characters is an amateur lepidopterist and sometime entomologist with a particular enthusiasm for moths. Kingsolver blends insect erudition into the story so well that her readers barely notice how much they are learning and how much learning was required to teach so well. No one is showing off here. The knowledge of moths is a bonus in service of the story.

This use of information and knowledge arises naturally and of necessity from the story. In order to understand the character and the world in which she lives, the reader needs to know about moths. Moth culture permeates the prose. We come to care about moths because we care about the character who cares about moths. We are there in the thick and particular concerns of that one woman in the same way as we are involved in the culture of marlin fishing in Hemingway's *The Old Man and the Sea*.

Form and Fiction—organization and structure

In organizing voice in the creation of fiction, once the writer has conceived of the germ of the story, and chosen the teller, then it is simply a matter of beginning and then obeying the rhythms of the story being told. In the event of having written the opening sentence, the author will either know or come to know the form his story is taking on.

In some sense the forms of fiction are merely an acknowledgment of the length of the story being told. If the story is told in its entirety in less than one page, then it is perhaps anecdotal. If more substantial than that, it might be referred to variously as a lyric paragraph, a snapshot fiction, or a post-card story. One anthologist called these one paragraph stories, 'sniglets.' Whatever they are called, they must satisfy the reader in the telling. Certain French-Canadian authors have made a high art out of snapshot fictions.

If a story is longer than a page or two, we begin to refer to it as a short story. And some short stories are as long as forty pages, while others adhere to a rough estimate of around ten to twenty pages. William Faulkner's story "The Bear" has been referred to both as a short story and a novella and it comprises a chapter in his novel, *Go Down Moses*.

The novella falls roughly between fifty and one-hundred pages.

Joseph Conrad's book, *Heart of Darkness*, is frequently referred to as a novella.

The novel, the trilogy, the tetrology, the series, the magnum opus, the twelve-book cycle, the body of work, Proust's *Remembrance of Things Past* and Canadian novelist Hugh Hood's twelve book work, the Spenser novels by Robert Parker, Conan Doyle's Sherlock Holmes stories, each reveal how fluid and only slightly helpful it is to call something by its name in the creation of fiction. If the word novel acknowledges only the number of pages, then how is it a useful word?

Short stories must do in roughly twenty pages what novels do in two hundred. There are matters of compression and economy of language which can only be learned through reading and practicing of craft.

An interesting illustration of the concerns of form might be had by reading W.P. Kinsella's short story, "Shoeless Joe Jackson Comes to Iowa," and then reading his novel, Shoeless Joe. Kinsella wrote the story first and was persuaded to expand upon it and thereby create the novel. Both the short story and the highly celebrated novel are much respected examples of their respective forms. In the writing of fiction whether the author is interested in writing popular fiction or in the creation of a work of literary merit, the best writing in both popular and literary fiction engages the reader and rewards the reader's attention. The patterns of meaning and expression are most successful when they are particular rather than general, when they are real rather than true, when they excite the five senses, engage the mind, the heart, the body, and the spirit of the reader in one surround.

It matters not whether the work is autobiographical or regional or feminist or moral or whether it makes the reader think large thoughts. It is neither a virtue nor a vice to be conservative in style, nor is it a virtue or a vice to be experimental. A good story need not end happily. It might be complex or simple, light-hearted or dark, full of flights of lyrical and surreal experience or mundane and quotidian in its concerns. What matters is that it be written well. That its voice be authentic. That it be true to itself in the telling.

The Dos and Don'ts of Writing Fiction

- Do the writing...better a glorious failure than a blank page

- Do give yourself permission to surrender to the tale in   t   h   e
telling...it matters not at all where it comes from, but rather that it
arrives

- Do have faith in your material...it need not be grand adventure to
be worthy of attention...a simple and insightful glimpse through
the crack in a door can be far more illuminating than the entire
involvement of a noisy deathsome battlefield

- Do make the writing real, vivid, clear and precise

- Do engage the five senses

- Do take care in your choice of the teller

- Do integrate the descriptive, narrative, dramatic and expository
voices

- Do be true to the tale in the telling

- Do write what you know about

  ...know what you write about

  ...write what you care about

  ...care what you write about

- Do listen and surrender

- Do pay attention to the particular and give the reader the world

- Do mind your language...every word is important...use the best and
most exact word...learn your world

- Don't allow anything to distract you from doing the writing...espe-
cially self-consciousness and doubt

- Don't leap into themes and abstractions

- Don't write purely to inform or teach the reader a lesson...fiction is
not persuasion...it is not a sermon

- Don't interfere with the story or lose faith in the reader's intelli-
gence

- Don't dislike your characters
- Don't rely upon adjectives or pretty writing to simply perfume the telling
- Don't over-is your writing...over-reliance upon variations on the infinitive 'to be' amount to lazy writing and tedious reading
- Don't rely only upon "said" to acknowledge the speaker in dialogue
- Don't be afraid of gentle emotion and small moments of human affection...and don't confuse sentimentality with true sentiment

There are no tricks, no short cuts, no absolutes...if the hand is moving follow it—if it isn't—either walk away in a gathering mood or stay put above the page in a patient and faithful silence—do whatever it takes to keep you there—read, stare out the window, stare at the wall, drink cold coffee, listen to the songbirds, measure the weather...set the hand in motion using the bricolage of an accidental day...believe that the writing of one good sentence is worth a nuisance ground of dross

"I have forced myself to begin writing when I've been utterly exhausted, when I've felt my soul as thin as a playing card, when nothing has seemed worth enduring for another five minutes... and somehow the activity of writing changes everything."

–Joyce Carol Oates, *Paris Review*

Writing Creative Non-Fiction

On first blush, the phrase creative non-fiction has the ring of an oxymoron. To the uninitiated it might seem there is perhaps surface contradiction between the idea of creativity and its suggestion of invention and the idea of non-fiction which is bound by the rigors of fact.

What distinguishes non-fiction and creative non-fiction— the discipline of sameness

For most genres of non-fiction there is a discipline of sameness. There exists a vocabulary agreed upon. Merit arises from a formulaic style. The reader and the author might have a sense of shared expertise. The last thing a reader of non-fiction requires is originality in presentation or innovation in voice and style. Rather, there is a learned commonality to the writing. The writer assumes the reader is reading because of a common interest and a desire to know. Non-fiction creates an expectation of accuracy, objectivity, clarity and simplicity. The dance of words is the last thing the reader expects. Perfuming the truth with inventive writing amounts to an irritation. It gets in the way and is contrary to the reason we are reading. The writer can assume within the readership, a shared desire to know.

Assuming Indifference-making the reader care

Excellence in creative non-fiction arises first and foremost out of the quality of the writing. Its primary merits are literary. The basic objective of creative non-fiction is to interest the disinterested and to write so well that the writing informs and engages the otherwise aggressively indifferent reader. The success of creative non-fiction is measured by the response of those readers who otherwise don't care about the subject the writer is writing about. In order to achieve this, the writer of creative non-fiction must serve two masters. The one requires a disciplined adherence to the facts. The other insists upon the delight of literary touches and the celebration of language.

Where the creative writer is limited only by the bounds of imagination; the creative non-fiction writer is limited by the need to be accurate and true to the facts. It might be said that the creative writer is creating; while the creative non-fiction writer is re-creating. The former is leaping out of experience in order to invent a simulation of the real; the latter is leaping into experience in order to reinvent the real. And yet they share the imperatives of literary merit.

The writer of non-fiction is required to achieve accuracy and strive for the appearance of objectivity. The writer of creative non-fiction is similarly required to achieve accuracy, but rather than objectivity, creative non-fiction involves subjectivity. In creative non-fiction the reader expects a reliable intimacy, informed opinion, insightful perception married to innovation in style.

The content of the best creative non-fiction engages, informs, illuminates, reveals, persuades, enlightens, provokes, changes, entertains, moves, touches, surprises, confirms, reminds, interests, and teaches the reader. It introduces the novel and renews the familiar.

Gathering Material—acquiring content:
observing, experiencing, remembering, researching

The primary tools of the writer of creative non-fiction are exactly the same as those of any writer. To see with a clear eye, to listen with care, to taste with a mature yet clean palate, to scent with a subtle and discerning sense of smell, to touch experience with the entire flesh and to be awake and alive in the world, these are the exigencies of all writers. To be prepared to look long enough to see. To listen long enough to hear. To taste and smell long enough to acquire, discern, distinguish, identify and describe. To touch the ever variant atmosphere and wake the flesh to feeling. To know the life in which we live. To imagine the past, experience the present and remember the future and gather in experience as apprehended and accurate and recreated through vivid expression in language.

Poet Margaret Avison opens her sonnet, "Snow" with this line: "Nobody stuffs the world in at your eyes." An informed, engaged and perceptive observer has the capacity for expert cognition and hyper-conscious involvement and acknowledgment. The writer must first be prepared to learn to perceive, apprehend and consider the world. Learning to look. Instructing the senses. Looking with new eyes. Cleaning the lenses. Acknowledging the filters we put between ourselves and the world. We must learn to see before we can say. We must engage the primary cognitive imagination before we entertain the possibility of recreating in language the experience of life once removed in the writing.

I once went for a walk in the woods on the old Talbot estate outside of St. Thomas, Ontario. It was a day in late February and I walked in the company of self-taught naturalist and fellow poet, Mike Wilson. Like most, I had walked such landscapes, on just such a day dozens of times before. What was different about this day was that I was in the company of someone qualified to show me the world I was looking at. Where in the past, I had set my own pace, Mike was teaching me patience, perseverance, tenacity, and clarity. Where I had been satisfied by absence and the simple pleasure of walking, he taught me how to pause, how to honour the wilderness with silence and reverent attentiveness. "Nature longs to reveal itself," was his way of putting it. "To the worthy," he might have added.

Over the course of our day together he was teaching me where to look. When to look. How to look. He did not need to tell me why. Either I understood that, or I was hopeless. Why reveal to the blind-hearted. I longed to see for the sake of seeing and so I surrendered to his guidance with open eyes.

He showed me the frost fronds of a hind's print and interpreted the pre-dawn trek of a deer. We examined the crimson blood spray of hare caught and reconstructed the rodent's struggle with a thorn. We found and considered the scat and tracked the journey of the herd. And when he spoke of eagles, they appeared as if conjured by their mention. He reminded me that the world is there to be seen if you simply learn how to look and how to become the patient perceiving and perceptive expert observer. This same Michael Wilson in addition to being an amateur naturalist and committed conservationist is also a hunter and a professional Lake Erie fisherman. He has become intimate with this particular patch of land and its environment. He looks to the ecology of a precious swale and knows the names of the animals who depend upon it for their life. He sees the hogback and can walk its rim to where the bald eagles nest. He can name the gyring hawks. He can interpret the sentinel crows and speak laughingly and affectionately in their vocabulary. "Crows love to swear," he says knowing they have set their vulgar and loudly imprecating guard against us. This place is worthy of perceiving well and truly. He does not surrender to progress which champions change and fails to notice or acknowledge what might be lost if this landscape is turned into a golf course. He is both a part of and apart from this place. He is doing what every writer must do. He is paying attention. And he has learned how to do so.

He would say he is simply observing the obvious. But obvious to whom? Obvious how? His observations are meticulous, informed and full of care. He honours the ecology by being in the moment. He is intimate and passionately involved. He knows the world of this small and very particular fallowing. He knows its seasons and sub-seasons. He observes its rhythms in ever-changing light. He can name and consider its flora and fauna, its geography, geology, its varieties of weather, its history, its pre-history and its tiny rhythms in small and large time.

His perception, perspective, and point of view is also betrayed by what he values. He sees the rare four-toed salamander and sees a thing worth protecting and preserving. He shows those who accompany him into this environment what he thinks is of value. His view is subjective and reliable, though his sense of meaning is coloured by that preconception. He expects agreement. In my case, he gets it. However, what is true for him is not necessarily true for everyone. More importantly, the writer of creative non-fiction might see with clarity and give the reader what is real and what results from looking well and leave the reader to decide what is true.

Another example of heightened cognition and shifting perspectives might be illustrated by discovering, acknowledging, examining and changing the filters we put between ourselves and the object of our observation.

My mother was attempting to show me a photograph she had recently discovered when she inherited a box of old family photographs after the death of her mother. The photograph in question had been taken of her realtives including her maternal great-grandmother a few months before my own grandmother's birth. It was a black and white picture of the family posing in front of the farmhouse. The sole purpose my mother had in mind was to point out and identify my ancestors so that I would be made aware of the names and faces of the people and so that I might learn my relationship with them.

I was in a mischievous mood and so I refused to allow her to carry through with her intention. Instead, I removed the filter of my mother's solitary concern and required us both to look and question with a more discerning eye. It was not that I didn't want to know the identity of the people, it was rather that I did not want to rush to judgment. "Let's linger a little longer on the less obvious things," I importuned. And my mother and father went along and indulged me just to keep the peace. We all looked to the photograph with the intention of inference. We focused on the fashion of the people, the length and direction of shadow, the state of the house in the background, the look of peripheral light, the flora and fauna, and the lazy dog on the grass, for we were seeking answers to such questions as, what time of day, what month, what seasons, what year, what affluence etc.

By looking with different perspective, by turning our attention to every available aspect and detail of the photograph, this particular photograph began to reveal itself in a variety of ways. By frustrating first intentions in the lookers, we arrived at a series of wonderful illuminations. We excited memories and talked of things long forgotten and rarely acknowledged.

My father suddenly remembered by having focused briefly on the ginger-bread architecture of the front porch of the house in the background that mother's uncle had stripped the house of its loveliest features and sold them off for money. This reminded us all of the eventual nature of the man who was but a little boy the day the photograph was taken. By looking deeply into the past with greater tenacity of observation, my father was able to excite a more meaningful memory concerning not only the identity, but also the nature of the people in the photograph. These people were thereby slowly coming to life as individuals.

My mother, by looking twice and by looking long with a new eye noticed the trumpet vine which was in full bloom. By her lingering over the photograph, she excited a childhood memory of their orange and fragrant beauty. She remembered herself and her sisters as children at her grandmother's on the May Sundays of their childhood. She recalled how they would pluck the lovely orange blooms and pretend to herald the angels and kings that populated their pretending. This material of memory was made available to her by simply looking closer, looking longer, and requiring herself to see. She was revivifying this dead drab black-and-white paper and revitalizing the spring of her own childhood.

As for me, what had begun as an exercise in teaching my mother and father to linger a little longer over the less obvious aspects of a photograph, resulting in bringing to life aspects of the photograph I had not anticipated. What for me had been a simple experiment in observation, for my parents became a journey which yielded long forgotten moments of their own past. This reveals one of the first sources of the material of non-fiction—the primary image. The cognitive experience. The educated perception.

The writer of creative non-fiction, in addition to being a reliable observer, must have the tenacity of mind to consider experience long enough to deepen and renew its meaning. The writer of creative non-fiction must be prepared to turn experience over in the mind long enough to see it for what it is. There is a quality of an ever-open, ever-receiving, ever-considering, ever-questing and ever-questioning mind. The writer is a seeker seeking to understand, refusing assumptions, questioning, asking the obvious and posing the surprising questions that no one else has thought to ask—the ones the narrow minded and timid and threatened by unsettling truths fear or refuse to ask. The riddle returns us to the unexamined or under-examined experience. The humbling familiar moments we renew by showing how thick with meaning even the simple moments are.

At the end of his life, the great mathematician Isaac Newton was asked how he saw himself. The brilliant genius replied that he saw himself simply as a boy turning pebbles on the beach. How ask the questions a child might ask? How achieve that humility and wonder? How acquire the perceptions and insights of the master combined with the insatiable curiosity of a child? This sensibility has the potential to yield the material of a true writer.

The writer of creative non-fiction must not only perceive reliably, experience deeply, profoundly and clearly, remember well and intimately, but also develop the skills of a scholar. Even private memory needs to be researched for it has the context of shared experience and the larger context of human experience. Perhaps we grew up during the war. Perhaps we were born in the depression. Perhaps we were profoundly moved by the death of a beloved president. Perhaps our sense of things has changed over time. Perhaps we were so powerfully influenced by the spirit of our own times that we almost forget to remind ourselves and our readers how it was for us.

There is a true story told me by a broadcaster. It concerns the early days of television and the first TV appearance of a Canadian Prime Minister. So the story goes, The Rt. Hon. Louis St. Laurent was scheduled to give a speech which was to be broadcast on TV. It seems the people of Montreal were so excited and pleased by the prospect that they hurried home from work and dressed up in their Sunday best, for fear of being seen by him in their living rooms. It seems they thought it possible that while they were looking in, he was looking out. It is hard to believe, especially in the urbane and sophisticated cosmopolitan Montreal, that there had ever been a time of such technological innocence. And yet it was true. And yet it occurred. And so we do indeed have a sense of things. We writers must never allow ourselves the luxury of forgetfulness or inaccuracy. The Roman statues were painted. The Vikings did not wear horned helmets. We were once amazed by television.

In honouring memory, in relating perception, in sharing experience, in doing the necessary research, in communicating knowledge, we must ask ourselves what do we know for certain, what do we think we know, what don't we know and how might we find out and come to know and finally how might we best write about these things?

One of the most interesting stories which I have ever had the privilege of unearthing and researching and telling began with a very simple question. My wife and I purchased a cottage on Lake Erie in the spring of 1989. The cottage was located in Peacock Point, a small community of only slightly more than one hundred mostly summer residences located on a cliff overlooking the north shore between Selkirk in the west and Nanticoke in the east. Because I agree with South African poet Stephen Watson who says that incuriosity is one of the greatest of human vices, I immediately set out to find out for myself where Peacock Point got its name.

So the simple question, 'what's in a name?' would prove to have a very difficult and time-consuming answer. When I asked my neighbours, 'where did Peacock Point get its name?' most of them were either indifferent, or only mildly curious or if they were deeply curious, they had no idea how to find out. The few who thought they knew were either partly or entirely wrong. Some speculated wildly about there having been peacock keepers at the lake. Some repeated rumours of pirates by the name of Peacock. They were repeating the misinformed local lore made available at the nearest museum. The most believable rumour involved a man by the name of Peacock who may or may not have been an American spy in the war of 1812 and who may or may not have been executed by the British for the crime of Treason. This latter rumour proved both the most likely and the most intriguing. How to find out?

I began with local histories including the late-nineteenth century County atlas of Haldimand-Norfolk. Therein was a reference to a man who squatted on the lake and made no improvement on the land and who when war broke out between United States and Canada in the summer of 1812 simply disappeared.

Like most writers with time, energy, and inclination and with the leisure and resources to do the research I became briefly obsessed. One of the most thrilling aspects of my quest involved the fact that I was the only person on the planet who currently cared enough to dig and dig and never surrender. Like most obsessive writers I became a bore and an enthusiastic expert of available information. And after focusing my attention for nearly two years on my quest, I discovered that there were two George Peacocks, a senior and a junior, that the father had arrived from America in 1807 with his wife and seven sons, that he was a blacksmith, that he squatted on the point of land which took his name, that he applied for and was refused land twice, that there was a warrant sworn out for his arrest just prior to the U.S. declaration of war, that Peacock Sr. had been tried and found innocent of the crime of disloyalty and that he had been released on his own recognizance and with assurance by neighbours who testified on his behalf that he would keep the peace, that he had fled immediately thereafter with his family into the United States, that he and his son George Peacock Jr. had returned to Canada with the invading Americans on October 9, under the leadership of William Sutherland, that he and his colleagues had engaged in smash-and-grab raids along the lake from Buffalo to Nanticoke where they were captured on November 13th at a skirmish referred to as 'The Battle of Nanticoke,' that George Peacock Sr. simply disappeared that night and was mostly likely one of four killed in the skirmish, and that his son George Peacock Jr. was captured that evening, sent to York Jail where he remained in a foul state for the entire winter, and from whence he was brought to trial at the Assize at the Union Hotel in Ancaster, that he was among 14 convicted of the crime of High Treason and sentenced to be hanged drawn and quartered, a sentence carried out in the shadow of Richard Beasley's house at what is now Dundurn Castle overlooking Burlington Bay in Hamilton. By doing the research, I became the only person on the planet who knew there were in fact two George Peacocks, a father and son. The danger of obsession and the perils of research arises from the assumption that our private enthusiasms are shared by all. Of course, the local people of Peacock Point had mixed feelings about the heritage of the name of their community. It wasn't a pirate. It was a traitor and a traitor's son. But why did this man risk everything in order to take up arms against his own former neighbours? Surely this was a tale of fascination, if not one which would flatter everyone, and most especially the guardians of local history and the descendants of the heroes of early Upper Canada, the United Empire Loyalists.

By digging deeply and never giving up, I was able to unearth the minutes of the trial. I am most proud of that since most true historians said they did not exist. I was able to bring to light two eye-witness accounts of the execution which was indeed both grisly and singular in nature since it was the only time such a sentence was carried out on North American soil and it was the last time it happened anywhere in the British Empire. The final story does not flatter anyone. It reveals self-interest and careerism and corruption and outright lying on the part of those involved. And it betrays a laziness on the part of most who have investigated the story at all.

A second story, yielded by this first arises from the fact that there was a man by the name of Joseph Willcocks who led a band of traitors to the Canadian cause calling themselves the Canadian Volunteers. When I was satisfied that I had exhausted the tell of Peacock's tale, I set out to find out more about this Willcocks especially since it has been so often misreported by historians that Peacock was a member of the Canadian Volunteers since he was not.

This Joseph Willcocks, an Anglo-Irish immigrant who arrived at York in Upper Canada in December of 1799 had a very interesting career. His brother Richard who had stayed at home in Ireland, was knighted by the crown for his contribution to the Muenster constabulary. Meanwhile, Joseph died in the Uniform of an American Lieutenant Colonel serving as the highest ranking officer in the occupying forces of the United States of America during their brief occupation of Fort Erie in the late summer of 1814. Willcocks had been the personal secretary of Peter Russell, the highest ranking political figure in Upper Canada. He had been friends with many of the most important men in York. He was a popularly elected member of the legislature. He had established the first political newspaper in Upper Canada. He had served as the Sheriff of the Home District. He was called upon by Isaac Brock to represent the military interests of Upper Canada with the Grand River Natives. He carried out that task as emissary despite serious personal ill health. He served with distinction and heroism as a gentleman volunteer at the battle of Queenston heights. He was acknowledged as ultra-loyal by his personal enemies. And then he went over to the other side and even went so far as leading the burning party which torched his home village of Newark where he had lived for nearly a decade. Why?

When despite his rank and authority, there was no mention whatsoever of his presence at Fort Erie during a re-enactment of the American occupation (remember he was the officer in charge of those forces) and I made inquiry, the local historian said, 'oh that story is just too complicated to tell.' And when I asked about him at a museum in Niagara-on-the-Lake the local historian there became so angry at the utterance of Willcocks' name that he almost leapt over the desk at me. This was a story! And it all began with a simple loose thread arising from an incredibly simple question, 'what's in a name?' and not being satisfied when I was lied to or when I was told 'the lie agreed upon' or when I was discouraged by difficulty. The story was there for the tenacious and obsessed writer.

Thus far this story has yielded three essays and two books. The essays tell the story as a narrative history. The books *Tongues of the Children* and the as-of-yet unpublished *In the Terrible Weather of Guns* are both examples of documentary poetry and semi-fictional prose. They involve a blending of fact and fiction fleshed out by the imagination.

This brings us to considerations of forms in creative non-fiction.

Form in creative non-fiction

Just as it is with other genres, creative non-fiction and literary journalism involve the complementary elements of content, form and style. The genres of creative non-fiction might suggest appropriate form. The autobiography, the journal, the memoir, the essay, the record, the exposé, the documentary poem, the narrative history, the biography, the article, the profile, the feature, the column each will result from the exigencies of the tale you have to tell. And each will suggest the format of presentation. And each may also in part be shaped by the place it is imagined for publication. Will the writing make its first and only appearance in a daily newspaper along with the other writing that dies with the day? Is it being written for a magazine, a journal, a literary quarterly, a web site, an anthology, or as part of an ongoing longer work which will result in a book? What are our intentions and what will be the result of those intentions? How do we perceive the work and in what format will it arrive in the readers hands?

Voice in Creative Non-fiction

In creative non-fiction the author's point of view is very important. Creative non-fiction tends towards a subjective, intimate, passionate and personal involvement in the story being told. Even where there is a pretended objectivity, the writer clearly cares about the subject of concern. The style of writing is meant to enhance the impact of the story. There is a clear and ever-present inner involvement on the part of the writer. There exits a vital, spontaneous, literary requirement in the prose voice. The voice must entertain, engage, persuade, inform and excite the reader. The perceptions must be fresh and spontaneous in both their content and expression. Consider for example, Anne Frank's simple observation, "paper is more patient than man." This brilliant and thoughtful coining of phrase lifts her diary above the quotidian and ordinary observation of many diarists. When Helen Keller said of safety, "safety is a superstition," she captured in those four words a new way of looking at a public obsession of every parent. When Marshall McLuhan wrote, "the medium is the message" he helped us to think about the way in which our interaction with the text is dependent upon the nature of presentation. And when he re-wrote the phrase as "the medium is the massage" he turned that idea on its head. When the writer Jeanne Marie Laskas wrote of perennials as 'plants that only pretend to die," she captured in those six words a fresh view. She makes her fellow writers wish they'd written that. Her phrase entertains, informs, reminds, renews, engages, inspires and makes the avid gardener return to the earth just a little amused and a touch amazed thinking, "I wonder why I never thought of it quite that way?" It's a matter of having the content, of shaping it into the best and most appropriate form and finding the perfect voice to tell it in. These are the same problems as those faced by the poet and the writer of fiction. Where non-fiction differs is in that it insists upon a scrupulous adherence to the facts.

The Dos and Don'ts of Writing Creative Non-fiction

See both the dos and don't of writing poetry and writing fiction—they apply as well to writing creative non-fiction.

- Do wake up and be alive in the world
- Do develop reliable, focused, clear and profoundly patient and perceptive powers of observation
- Do learn and develop the research skills of a tenacious and reliable scholar. Read all the secondary sources, but more importantly, go to the primary sources and dig until you find them all.
- Do be curious and remain open and ever-seeking in your quest to know
- Do spend the necessary time and expend the necessary energy to exhaust all possible avenues of knowing. Remember the page is patient. Unless you have a real deadline, the blank page can wait you out.
- Do become aware of the filters you put between yourself and the world. Be aware of your bias and acknowledge your perspective lest it betray you and blind you.
- Do be accurate and scrupulously true to the facts.
- Do learn the language of your concern and use that language well when it serves your subject.
- Do be subjective, intimate and passionately involved and develop a self-inclusive point of view.
- Do engage in an innovative and original style which serves and enlivens the subject of your concern.
- Do write for yourself first. Like the author of fiction, be your own first audience.
- Don't ever allow yourself the luxury of laziness or incompetence in research. If you don't know, find out. If you don't know how to find out, find out how to find out. And examine all your own assumptions.

- Don't ever surrender to the daunting task of "too much work". If you find yourself saying, that's too hard, then the story isn't yours to tell. The reader of creative non-fiction is unforgiving of a lazy mind.

- Don't be afraid to tell the hard truths. There is nothing flattering about falsity or half-truth. Honesty is not a weapon when it is relevant, necessary and employed in the spirit and service of helpful, meaningful and healing truth.

How to Get Published

A lmost every writer who has ever put pen to paper imagines the day when his or her writing will appear in print. From the very first serious piece of writing I ever created, I found myself dreaming my work as it might appear in book form with my name emblazoned on the cover. I fantasized finding myself on the shelf in a bookstore and in the stacks of the library under L for Lee. I conjured amazement and admiration on the faces and in the minds of a phantom readership. I conceived of the praise of family and friends as they held my writing in their hands. I saw my work honoured and transformed by strangers. And I thank my lucky stars that publications did not happen too early. I thank goodness that I am not haunted by any permanent and publicly available widely distributed examples of juvenalia. Premature publication might have stunted my journey on the long apprenticeship towards becoming the best writer it was in me to become? Thank goodness I had the opportunity to evolve and learn and grow and improve as an author learning to achieve readiness before the opportunity to publish widely presented itself. Oh, I gladly would have leapt the queue if anyone had offered to publish my work before it was worthy of attention. Thank goodness no one ever made the offer.

Achieving Readiness

Walk into any book store. Stand in the stacks of any major library. Look around. Take in the competition. Ask yourself what you must do to be worthy of reader attention. What must you do to become the best writer it is in you to become. Realize that the competition is stiff. Recognize that the requirement is excellence in both content and presentation.

If you want to get published, get good. If you wish to be worthy of ideal reader attention, learn your craft. Only then do you honour your imaginary reader. If you aspire to publication, then become worthy of publication. Serve the long apprenticeship. Achieve voice, originality, authority, excellence.

Better a messy masterpiece in a drawer for future generations to discover as a posthumous delight than a beautifully presented mediocrity to be savaged by critics, half-read by strangers and sold at a yard sale or left unpurchased and unread in a dust bin. Better wait to honour the next piece of writing than insist upon publishing that which might live to embarrass you.

So, the first real step in your journey to getting published involves learning to await readiness, learning to recognize readiness when it occurs, learning to look forward to the future moment when you might look back without regret upon your first published work.

If you are easily satisfied and desperate to see your work in print, then you might seek and find a vanity press. Or you might join a group of fellow authors who publish a journal or a year-end anthology of their own writing. Anyone with enough money can participate in such a venture.

If you simply wish to be published, there are hundreds of presses willing to print your work for cash. It is only a matter of tracking them down, negotiating a price, paying for the production costs, warehousing the books and then marketing, distributing, promoting and selling the product yourself. You may find certain outlets willing to take such product on consignment. You might host a self-created event and launch your work.

The work produced by self-publication need not be sub-standard in its production value. Neither does it need to be weak or inferior in content. Many well-established authors have resorted to self-publication. We live in an environment where there are many more manuscripts aspiring to publication than there are opportunities to be published. The fact that a manuscript is rejected by a publisher is not certain evidence that the manuscript in question is unworthy. Indeed, publication in and of itself is never proof positive of excellence.

Getting Published

In the contemporary world the idea of what being published means is changing. As for me, I am for the most part a poet and as such I have had work published in the traditional formats such as journals, anthologies, magazines, newspapers, periodicals, and books. In addition to this, my work has been broadcast on radio and performed on television. It has been published as electronic text as part of an e-zine on the internet. It has been made into a video. It has been performed on stage and on the radio as part of a radio documentary. It has been published as part of a window-display anthology. It has been printed on T-shirts, and made into posters and post cards. It has been published on CD ROM and appeared on the side of a city bus and on the subway wall. It has also been prepared and presented as part of an ecphrasic project as an interactive work-in-progress appearing on a web site.

My first poem was published in a high school year book. And as I learned my craft over the writing of unpublished poems, I began to publish more widely, first in student-edited journals at University, and then ever-more widely in journals, periodicals and anthologies building up to the publication of my first book.

So, if you wish to publish, I would advise that you start locally. Think small and be cautious and at least temporarily satisfied and indeed even thrilled with the lifeline of the close at hand. Publish within your community. Find the available outlets for your work. Join the local writers' group. Don't look to go too far too fast.

If you are persuaded by that advice to patience, then you might ask which work you might honour and how you might do that.

Choosing Your Own Best Work—the art of self-editing

Learning to recognize, edit and select your own best work is an art in and of itself. As mentioned previously, it is part of the writing process.

The most reliable judgment arises when you give the work time to mature and you give yourself the time to distance yourself from the first blush of inspiration which gave rise to the writing. That involves letting the thrill of creation wear off. Let the finished work sit for a while and ask yourself in a week if you still admire it. Then ask the same of yourself in a month, in a season, in a year, and so on. This does not guarantee excellence, but it does increase the likelihood that the work in question might rank in the first order.

When you have arrived at those first pieces of writing which rise above the page and sustain their quality within the scrutiny of your own best judgment, then you might have something worthy of publication. It is then that you need to proof read, edit, polish and perfect the work with a final and rigorous re-write.

Make a perfect copy of that final best draft. Assume weak eyes in bad light. Assume the reliable judgment of demanding strangers. Choose a clean font, black-inked on fresh absolutely clean white paper. Demand maximum legibility that flatters, but does not crowd the page.

What to send, How to send, Where to send, When to send

You can put a tie on a pig, but it doesn't make him a man. Better a messy masterpiece than a pretty mediocrity. Better yet, a masterpiece which also achieves a presentational perfection. The masterpiece is challenging to achieve. Presentational excellence is easy. Anything less than excellence in presentation amounts to an insult to both the reader and the work.

What to send:

- Send only your best work. Send it only after you have honoured it with both self-critical editing and presentational perfection.
- Send exactly the right amount of work to satisfy the requirements of the destination.

How to send:

- Find out the format required by the publisher to whom you are sending your work.

- Mail a manuscript when a hard copy is requested. Include a disk in the correct format where required. E mail when e mail is requested. E mail as an attachment in the format required by the publisher. Always include a clear, concise cover letter with the essential information. Always include a stamped, self-addressed envelope for returning your work.

Where to send:

- Send your work only to publishers appropriate to the style, form and content of the work in question. Familiarize yourself with the destination of your work. Subscribe to the journals to which you are sending. Read the Market guides. Visit the library. Ask yourself why an acquisitions editor would be in the least bit interested in anyone who was not willing to put forward the effort to learn about the nature of the publication in which the writer in question aspired to publish. For example, if you want to publish in *Fiddlehead*; then subscribe to *Fiddlehead*, or at the very least, read several issues of the magazine and become aware of the sort of work appearing therein.

The best way to ensure the maximum likelihood of your success in placing your work is to have the right work arrive in right hands at the right destination at the right time.

When to send:

- Most journals and most publishers have a season when the work might most likely receive a sympathetic reading. Find out when that is. Either purchase and read the most helpful and informative books of the trade or visit the library and consult the most up-to-date market guides.

Organizations for Writers

There are many organizations for writers. Some are particular to discipline. Some have membership requirements. Some are open to all who apply. A writer should become familiar with the organizations to which he or she might belong and there are definite benefits arising from belonging not the least of which arises from simply being part of a community of like-minded people.

By consulting a trade book, you might find out what these organizations are.

Useful books

One of the most comprehensive guides to the Book trade in Canada is published annually by Quill and Quire. It is called—*Quill and Quire: The Book Trade in Canada*—Your Complete guide to the Canadian Publishing Marketplace. It contains the names and addresses and a brief summary of important information on publishers, agents, organization, and awards in the Canadian book industry. There are other equally useful books of the same kind such as *The Canadian Writers Market Guide: the official handbook of the Canadian Authors Association.*

It is certainly helpful to consult such a guide in order to prepare your work for submission for consideration for publication. However, this is no substitute for becoming familiar with the publisher to whom you may wish to send your work. You should honour the destination of your work by honouring the publisher with your attention. Read the journal. Read the books published by the publisher. Don't flatter with false flattery. Honour with honest attention.

The Dos and Don'ts on How to Get Published

- If you want to get published; get good.
- If you want to get published; learn your craft.
- If you want to get published; do the very best writing it is in you to do. Honour your first reader with excellence.

What does 'getting published' mean

In the contemporary world opportunities for getting published are more various and wide-ranging than ever before. If by getting published you mean having your work made available in a widely distributed format, then that is a very great ambition indeed. You might begin by being more easily satisfied. Publish locally. Publish in small ways. And build a career. Begin in the foreground and work your way up and out into a broader market.

Getting Published: preparing and perfecting the manuscript for presentation

- Do evaluate the content

  —engage your own true, honest, most self-critical evaluation of readiness: ask yourself—is this in its entirety the very best work of which you are capable

  —seek the reliable and helpful opinion of those most qualified to make expert improvement on your work and give serious consideration to their advice

  —proof read to perfection

  —self-edit for excellence

  —polish for appearance and

  —produce a perfect final draft

Presentation

- Do assume weak eyes in bad light
- Do choose a font whose size and style both maximize legibility and minimize decorativeness
- Do achieve a clear, dark script well-inked, one side only, on clean 8 1/2 by 11 white paper with a professional weight and gauge
- Do honour the presentational paradigms of content, mode and genre

  For Poetry: one poem per page single spaced with a style that acknowledges titles and maximizes the clarity of verse divisions of each poem

  For Prose: all prose should be double spaced and true to the conventions of form and genre

Honouring a stranger—your first reader

- Do help your first reader to apprehend as quickly, clearly, and precisely as possible the nature of your submission by writing a standard cover letter which is dated; correctly and comprehensively addressed; and which contains with brevity and clarity only the absolutely essential information. In producing a cover letter, scrupulously adhere to the standard format of a proper letter.

Increasing the likelihood of success

There are no guarantees that the acquisitions editor will recognize and honour excellence with acceptance. However, you can increase the likelihood of success by sending—1—the right work to —2—the right person/(first reader/acquisitions editor/publisher) at —3—the right time.

1. By the right work, I mean the best and most appropriate work for the publisher in question.

2. By the right person, I mean that individual who will receive, read, notice and honour your work. It is absolutely necessary that you become knowledgeable about the nature of the publication to which you are sending and the publisher to whom you are making a submission.

3. By the right time, I mean that you must become aware of the publisher's policy and predicament. Every journal and every publishing house has a season and a period during which your work has an optimum opportunity of receiving potentially beneficial attention.

• Do be prepared to wall paper a very large room with rejection slips.

• Do be prepared to re-consider the readiness and appropriateness of the work you are submitting.

• Do familiarize yourself with the publishing industry and with the publications to which you are making submission. Ask yourself why they would be interested in you if you are not sufficiently interested in them.

• Don't get discouraged. Don't give up writing. Do pick yourself up. Dust yourself off. Keep writing. You're only wasting your time if you give up.

Part II

Sending Yourself
to the
School of Yourself

A series of practical exercises
in writing

I am calling this section of the book *Sending yourself to the School of Yourself* because it is my conviction that in the long apprenticeship each aspiring writer might learn what he or she needs to know on his or her own. A writer might toil in solitude by reading as a writer reads and by writing at every opportunity.

That said, I also believe that a writer's journey might be both accelerated and clarified by the reading of a practical book on the craft of writing and by the practice of 'exercises' which focus the writer's attention on an aspect of craft.

Each of the exercises in *Sending Yourself to the School of Yourself* has been writer tested and used in classrooms with much success across North America. It is my belief that no exercise is too primary, nor too sophisticated for a participant to learn something from the doing of the thing. Nothing is quite so destructive to the process as arrogance. Arrogance disqualifies the learner.

I have used each of the exercises herein with participating writers from the earliest stages of development all the way through to the most advanced in both age and accomplishment. My personal philosophy arises from the conviction that if we surrender to the learning surely it will teach us something.

On the other hand, I do not expect that an attempt at any of the following exercises will result in great writing. If any participant achieves the accident of great writing, then he or she is most fortunate. Rather than the achieving of great writing, the exercises herein are designed to explore aspects of writing and to focus attention upon experiments in aspects of craft. The cross-fertilization between the writer's own work and the work resulting from the exercises herein is the main intention of each and every exercise.

In addition to being a useful program of 'experiment and learning' for the aspiring writer, the following exercises are also useful tools for the teacher of creative writing.

Here follow the 6 stages of the six-part process for using the exercises in *Sending Yourself to the School of Yourself.*

The process

1. **Read before you write:** if you are writing haiku, it is essential to study a few professional haiku asking yourself or the students two very simple questions: What is this thing? and how was it made?

2. **Do the writing:** produce a first draft. During the creative process you need not worry about neatness, spelling, or even self-editing. The idea is to get the work done.

    If the object of the lesson is to follow instructions, then insist upon it. If the object of the lesson is to accomplish the best piece of writing possible on any given day then I am guided by a single simple instruction. If I send you into the kitchen to make an apple pie and you make a pumpkin pie, can you still eat it? And if you make a mud pie, you can also eat that as children drink imaginary tea from empty service.

3. **Edit the work:** reconsidering the first draft: at this point the individual student should be encouraged to make certain that every aspect of the piece of writing is as it should be. That means checking spelling, making line breaks where they should be, being absolutely certain that every word counts...etc.

4. **Polish and perfect: producing a final draft**: this takes editing one step further. Push the piece of writing to the limits of its possibilities. The teacher must always be guided by a simple principle. The piece of writing belongs to the author. Any changes, however persuasive, must remain up to the individual.

5. **Produce a good final copy**: the student should be encouraged to have at least one clean, legible, perfect final copy of the work. Ideally that means not so much as a smudge. Assume weak eyes in bad light. Be sure to keep all drafts of original work. Every step along the way is equally important.

6. **Share**: Reading* and Listening** if the work is worth writing, then it is worth sharing.

   *Reading aloud is a form of interpretation, and it needs to be taught, learned and practiced.

   **Listening is an activity. As writers we need to be trained to listen well. Editing others can be very instructive in learning the art of self-editing. Encouraging questions or comments helps to ensure learning.

   Be prepared to revise based upon reader/audience response. Hold your ground where it deserves to be held. Revise the writing where it doesn't work. And always be weary of the difference between the response to the written and the performed or spoken word. An audience and a reader are very different creatures indeed.

Stop Making Sense:
exercises in writing poetry

I am calling this section 'stop making sense' because creative endeavors require that we free ourselves from conventions of ordinary thinking. In school we learn to think clearly, logically and discursively. The writing of poetry and certain types of creative fiction and non-fiction returns us to the freedom of thinking like children. In so doing, we must give ourselves permission to play, to explore, and to make brave leaps into the unknown.

Blurring

Blurring is a technique whereby you put yourself in a frame of mind in which the writing might get done. If you are fortunate enough to be inspired, then you need no artificial stimulation to get you to the place where you might write without impediment. On the other hand, if you find yourself in a situation where you are required to write and you are not in the mood, or where you wish to write but you are without ideas, then you might simply give yourself permission to write through the garbage accepting the possibility that you might overcome the inertia which plagues you and thereby arrive at a point where the true writing begins.

By blurring, I mean the mental activity where you deliberately mishear conversations, misread words and let your pen begin to stray into unexpected territory of simply writing whatever occurs. Ignore the results and simply follow the flow of what you are writing. Surrender to the task of getting words on the page.

Bricolage

Another way of overcoming a writer's block on a given day or within the context of an exercise, is to simply take whatever is at hand. Use the environment in which you find yourself to provide you with the content of your writing. Take note of the time of day. Write the room. Write the weather at the window. Write the permanent and accidental objects and events as they occur around you. Write the sounds, sights, scents, ambience and flavour of your surroundings. Take this one's socks and that one's shoes, this one's hair colour and that one's frock. Construct and capture what you see, feel, hear, taste and smell. Become an object. Become the wind. Do the writing. Give in to the activity of putting words upon the page. If you're lucky, you might capture the day in passing. If you're lucky you might leap beyond the day and find yourself in territory beyond the immediate and close at hand. Whichever is the case, at the very least you will have written something. You will have overcome the silence.

if you boil a watch...

The first exercise is meant to free the writer from the need for slavish adherence to logic. It is not meant to suggest the need for deliberate obscurity. Needless obscurity is a vice of bad writing. On the other hand playfulness and mischief are often the delight at the centre of the less than obvious connection between very disparate things. Incongruity is the heart of laughter. Interconnectedness is the soul of metaphor.

What is a poem?

Using this title, complete the following poem and then read the poems on the next pages:

> *If you boil a watch*
> *and time it with an egg*
> *what do you get?*

If you boil a watch
and time it with an egg

what do you get?

a geranium

*

If you boil a watch
and time it with an egg

what do you get?

an angry jeweler
a disappointed hen

*

If you boil a watch
and time it with an egg

what do you get?

a poached Timex
on toast

*

If you boil a watch
and time it with an egg

what do you get?

apologies from a foolish cook

*

If you boil a watch
and time it with an egg

what do you get?

an extraordinary breakfast.

If you boil a watch
and time it with an egg

what do you get?

a straight jacket vacation
puzzled looks
in a lonely diner

thirty seconds to change your
mind

hot to the elbow

Monday morning to Friday night
November
7 o'clock   forever

an angry hour
till your watch is dry
as an old pen writing a new poem

*

If you boil a watch
and time it with an egg

what do you get?

two faces
one face on the boil
one boil on the face
*

If you boil a watch
and time it with an egg

what do you get?

time to eat

*

If you boil a watch
and time it with an egg

what do you get?

if you swim in the sky
    and fly in the sea

if you drink the wind
    on a thirsty day

if you hold the moon
    in an open mind
like a clabber of cheese
    with a face of light

if you swallow the sun
like a lamp with a shade

you'll be the blue
of a beautiful day
like an egg
with and face and two hand
unborn.

    Here is a poem by a elementary school student reprinted here with
permission from the author:

If you boil a watch
and time it with an egg
what do you get?
You get an angry triceratops.
A burnt ladybug.
A fed up horse.
A ratty old hat.
An angry owner.
An ant celebration.

—by Alisha Hill

Sound Poetry

Poetry began in the oral tradition. In the tradition of the spoken word, the following exercises arise from the traditions of heightened utterance and the presentational mode where poems are written to be spoken aloud. Rather than writer and reader the works in this section imagine a performer and an audience, a speaker or multiple speakers and a listener or an audience of listeners. In the more experimental works, sound poetry arises from the most playful babble. In the words of professional sound poet Penn Kemp, "Sound poetry is the last resort for creative expression when words fail the enormity of emotions." In a more conservative vain, a sound poem might simply be a poem written for reading aloud. It might be quite conventional or extremely wild and liberating. It might arise from that place where language and music meet in a variety of rhythmic vocalizations. It might employ a single voice or be a choral piece of multiple voices. It might begin in the giddy glossolalia of invented language or in the same way as a conventional poem. Sound poetry celebrates the human voice and emphasizes the poem as performance piece.

One of the easiest ways to explore sound poetry is through the use of the alphabet. You might choose a theme and write an alphabet chant such as the following poem:

Making a Man: The Frankenstein Project
       and armpits and adam's apple
and buttocks...biiiiiig buttocks
and collar bone clavicle
and duodenal loop
and elbow elbowing and epiglottis
and feet
and gluteus maximus and goood gumms

and hard head and healthy heart and huge HANDS

and ileum and isles of langerhorn
and just-about-a-hundred-yards-of-skin
and k/nocking k/nees & k/nocking k/nuckles
and lips, luscious lips

and mumblemouthmumblemouthmumblemouth
and nose with nostrils nostulating
and only one opinionated medulla oblongata
and pupils and solar plexus
and quite a lot of hair
and ribs
and skeleton and pyloric sphincter
and teeth
and uvula hanging down
and very very very very very smart brain
and wrists
and X-ray vision like Superman
and yesterday he wasn't alive but today he is because he's the

Frankenstein project
and with zillions
and zillions
and zillions and zillions of years to live.

Doggerel

Doggerel is light verse which is often comic in intent. The word doggerel in English poetry refers to the light verse which employs easy rhyme and facile rhythm of the sort used in the creation of limericks, children's verses and comic poetry. Although often used as a pejorative in description of bad poetry, the word was first used by the English poet Chaucer to describe his own work. Doggerel is a word of indeterminate ancestry. It most likely goes back to the scorn of such phrases as dog-Latin and dog-rhymes resulting in the diminutive doggerel. Like 'sound poetry' it is most effective and delightful when read aloud. The exercises in the writing of doggerel are both playful and liberating and helpful in developing the skills for the writing of more serious formal verse.

Follow the following formula in the creation of a series of light verse poems.

Of All the Fishes in the Sea

1. Of all the fishes in the sea
2. I wish I were a **shark**
3. So I could climb
4. Up on a rock
5. And there I'd learn to **bark.**

*

Of all the fishes in the sea
I wish I were a **sturgeon**
So I could climb
Up on a rock
And learn to be a **surgeon.**

*

Of all the fishes in the sea
I wish I were a **pike**
So I could climb
Up on a rock
And sing into a **mike.**

Now write one or two of your own:

Of all the fishes in the sea
I wish I were a...
So I could climb
Up on a rock
And...

*

1. Of all the animals in the woods
2. I wish I were a **bear**
3. So I could lie
4. Beneath a tree
5. And sleep without a **care.**

*

Of all the animals in the woods
I wish I were a **bunny**
So I could lie
Beneath a tree
When it is warm and **sunny.**

*

Of all the animals in the woods
I wish I were a **fox**
So I could lie
Beneath a tree
Among the sticks and **rocks.**

*

Now write one or two of your own:

Of all the animals in the woods
I wish I were a...
So I could lie
Beneath a tree
And...

*

1. Of all the birds up in the sky
2. I wish I were a **robin**
3. So I could sit
4. Down on a branch
5. And keep my tail a **bobbin'**.

*

Of all the birds up in the sky
I wish I were a **jay**
So I could sit
Down in a nest
And stay that way all **day**.

*

Of all the birds up in the sky
I wish I were a **crow**
So I could sit
Down on a branch
And "Caw" until you **go**.

*

Now write one or two of your own:

Of all the birds up in the sky
I wish I were a...
So I could sit
Down on a branch
And...

*

Of all the people in the world
I'm glad that I am **me**
So I can sit
Down at my desk
And write my **poetry**.

*

Of all the people in the world
I'm glad that I am **John**
So I can play
My own guitar
And sing my own sweet **song**.

*

Now you try one of your own:

Of all the people in the world
I'm glad that I am me
(*now finish this 5 line poem*)

*

Of all the people in the world
I'm glad that I am   (*your name*)
(*now finish this five line poem*)

Here are some first line ideas:

- Of all the beavers in the pond
  (and you might even try a seasonal poem)

- Of all the horses in the barn

- Of all the cats inside the house Of all the reindeer on the roof

- Of all the jobs within the town I'm glad my nose is red

- Of all the poems in this book I'll light my way

- Of all the thoughts inside your head On Christmas night

- Of all the feelings that I feel While you're asleep in bed.

The possibilities of this five line form are endless:

Of all the coffee in the world
I think I'm in your cup
Cause when you put
Your lips on me
*You drank me **bottom's up**.*

*

Of all the horses in the barn
I'm glad that I am Trigger
But my little stall
Is oh so small
Please make the stable bigger.

*

Of all galoshes in your house
I'm glad that I am yours
But if you slip me
On inside
Please wear me out of doors.

*

Of all the houses in the street
I'm glad you live in me
But did you notice
Where you are?
You're living in a tree.

*

Of all the poems in this book
This poem it is mine.
I wrote it with
A pencil stub
When I was ninety-nine.

*

The limerick is an easy form to imitate provided you internalize the rhythm of the form...da da-da, da da-da,

>
> *da-da:da da-da,*
> *da da-da, da-da*
> *da da-da da-da*
> *da da-da da-da*
> *da da-da, da da-da, da-da*

with an aa bb a rhyme scheme thus...

>
> *There once was a fellow named Lee*
> *Who wrote such bad poetry*
> *His verses were horrid*
> *And so were abhorred*
> *But that didn't stop ol' John B.*

and you can break the formula once you've mastered it...

> **There once was a fellow named Donne!**

>
> *There once was a fellow named Donne*
> *Who finished his limerick line one.*
> *He lied.*

*

>
> *There once was a fellow named Lou*
> *Who finished his limerick line two.*
> *He lied as well.*

*

>
> *There once was a fellow named Lee*
> *Who finished his limerick line three.*
> *That just wouldn't do*
> *To finish line two.*
> *That wouldn't be good poetry.*

Where Words Go

All the best written poetry pays close attention to the placing of words on the page. Poetry has an immediate recognition factor. It looks a certain way because it is a visual artifact. Fan the pages of a poetry anthology and you need not read a single word therein to know that you hold in your hands a collection of poems. The line breaks and stanza breaks have an instant familiarity to the experienced reader. A close reading of carefully crafted poetry reveals a relationship between the meaning and the form. The line breaks provide an opportunity for the creator to place a powerful emphasis on the last word in the line. The spaces ghost a silence and construct a white pause. The typeface and punctuation offer another opportunity for emphasis and meaning. Look to the wonderful poem by e.e. cummings, variously referred to as "in just spring" or as "Chansons Innocentes" and you will see a masterful and experimental use of typology and punctuation with a tight connection to meaning.

Perhaps the most obvious visual impact in poetics is that employed by those who compose what are called, "Concrete Poems". Concrete poetry is first and foremost a picture. In the most dramatic examples the poem creates a picture which might be framed and hung upon a wall to be looked at the way we might consider a painting or a photograph. Because it employs language in the creation of the picture, a deeper understanding of the meaning of the poem is available to the reader upon reading the work.

Canadian concrete poet bp nichol's famous poem, Love Evol is visually stunning and with its hint of demonism makes ironic mischief of human love and provokes thought.

Earle Birney's swirling eddying cursive with the word rock at the centre reveals the way handwriting might be employed in service of meaning.

Steven McCaffery's simple poem, **TUnnnEL**, reveals how simplicity and high concept can yield delight. George Swede's poem, THIIIEF m ss ng gives further evidence of this same principle.

Concrete poetry can also be quite complex, highly artistic, or conceptual. It can be employed as a technique within the context of a less visually experimental poem. It can also be visually mimetic as in the case of poems where the words are simply imitative of the shape of the subject about which they are written.

The more inventive, the more playful, the more insightful and visually inspired, the better the work. Personally, I'm not much of a practitioner of this kind of poetry because of my limited ability as a visual artist. But thinking of the poem as a visual object can be very liberating and indeed essential to the creation of free verse which pays heed to the look of the work and to the impact it has as a visual artifact.

asking the big questions

b b

or not

bb

Aspiring and apprentice poets often forget the fact that in free verse and in formal verse an emphasis in meaning can be achieved by taking care where the line breaks come. The poem need not be obviously pictorial for the poet to take care in the placing of the words upon the page.

The poem "October Trees" provides both a formula for experimenting with where words go as well as a clear rationale for taking care.

October Trees

Late October trees   (what?)
stand   (doing what?)
in the street   (where?)
    like lonely old men   (simile/comparison)

tired
    of
        the

        w   i   n   d.

First, let us consider the reason for the placing of the words. The title makes the subject of the poem clear. The season is autumn. The central image of the poem involves trees, most likely deciduous trees or that it to say trees that lose their leaves and are thereby most effected by the season.

The first word in the poem takes on power in that it adds to the information provided by the title. In late October the deciduous trees would be for the most part rather bleak, devoid of colour and denuded of their leaves.

The word "stand" stands alone and emphasizes a sense of isolation and solitude.

In the street establishes a village, town or cityscape. The street is the location where houses are established. So these trees are clearly in the midst of a community. Isolation set against the presence of others makes the solitude all the more dramatic.

The line to which the trees are compared is set to the side, thus emphasizing isolation and making the simile apt and making the shape of the poem a complement to the metaphor. The trees are like lonely old men in that they seem aged by autumn and the loss of their leaves. The suggested greyness is atmospheric. And the line itself is set to the side in the same way that the elderly might feel sidelined by life.

The last four words take on power in that they are each alone on a line. And they drift like the falling of leaves in the wind. If the reader reads the white space, the fatigue of the line invades the reading. It is thereby made imitative of the meaning of the words.

This poem is constructed to highlight the connection between the placing of words upon the page and the very meaning of the words which are being placed. The shape of the poem complements the content of the poem. The poem also provides a formula for creation.

One can also explore the relationship between the poem and visual art by creating a collage of images as a complement to the poem.

Various Exercises in the Free Verse Lyric

Free verse refers to poetry which is free from the formal strictures of end-line rhyme and a repeated rhythm or meter. That is not to suggest that free verse is entirely free. The lyric or descriptive free verse poem is not simply prose broken into lines and stanzas. As stated in the chapter on writing poetry, free verse celebrates the sound of words. As the child quoted in that chapter said, "poetry is when words sing."

Each of the exercises in this section begins with a formula or recipe and moves away from the formula into a freer exploration of the poetics involved in creation of a poem. One of the purposes of each exercise is to emphasize an aspect of poetry writing which might be carried over into an author's private projects.

Five Senses Writing

We live in a world which is increasingly dominated by one or two of the five senses. We watch movies. We watch television. We listen to the radio. We listen to music. And yet in writing we have an opportunity and indeed a responsibility to excite all five senses. The best writing takes advantage of this opportunity where it is appropriate and lives up to this responsibility where it is required. If you read as a writer reads, paying attention to the way a piece of writing is made, you will notice that the most admired writers honour this aspect of their craft. When we read a passage of description we are made to feel, taste, smell, see and hear the experience being written about. This exercise in 'five senses writing' provides a formula which requires the author to practice using the entire cognition in writing.

Here is the formula. For the first effort, include the actual words in the exercise:

I am

I hear

I see

I taste

I touch

I smell

I am

I am a Farmer's Son

I am a farmer's son
I hear the cattle lowing
on the morning wind
I see the cows
swing their milky udders
for the barns
I feel the ache of waking early
I taste the bacon smoke rising
from the coffee-scented air
I touch the cold linoleum
with bare feet
I am a farmer's son
    *

I am a Poet

I am a poet
I hear the silence
I see the brilliant winter white
 of an empty page
 greying in the glare
I taste cold coffee
 bitter in the cup
I smell the quiet ozonated rain
 the lemon oil resin of my cherry desk
 the lead and wood of shaven pencils
I feel the curl of my pen
 in my hand
 crawling its cursive over paper
I hear the silence
 filling with my quiet inner voice
 the voice of my heart
 the voice of my whispering breath
I am a poet

 *

Now write the poem and remove the lines, I hear, I taste, I smell, I see, I touch...

I am a Hockey Player

I am a hockey player skating
the perfect shining oblong egg
of new ice
under bright lights
I am sweating among men
skating hard
in Zamboni fumes
lost in the ack ack
of their blades
and the cut rush of practice before play

that spoils the surface
as a knife would spoil glass
and I am here with the slap of each stick
cracking the puck
so it bangs the boards
like cannon fire
or bangs the glass with the echo
of glass and hard-edged booms
or flies to the flag
or scars the wincing portrait of the queen
my muscles pull
against motion
pull inside my jersey
against the motion of myself
moving
in this rough ballet
...then saltily I am
sitting, saltily saying
the fact
of my being here and alive
on the slivery bench
in the woody walk about
of being a player
in love with this game
in love with this very game, for
I am a hockey player...

Try throwing your voice beyond the obvious...

I am all Days

I am all the days and hours
of the week in the world.
I am
the colour of dreams.
The salt-scatter light

in the black cloth of night.
I am Monday morning
waking
with the ache of slow breathing
like buttered dough in perfect heat.
I am Friday evening
in the beer-golden afternoon
and the midnight moon
clabber cheese and gouda white.
I am
all day Saturday
green-lawned and minted with cut grass
I am Sunday
lying in the sleep-late
of a coffee maker's gasping
with heavy books dead birding the floor
I dive into those pond deep places
that flow like clean oil
from an opening
in a blue bottle
I am the endless looping hours
at rest
in the rose-lazy trellis closing
well away from the fog-smoky week.

Note the use of all five senses in the following piece of writing taken
from my book, *Variations On Herb.*

The Boy with the Duck on His Head

The boy is five, running for the farmhouse with a duck on his
head. The duck is flapping his wings, beating the boy's ears,
hauling at his scalp like a storm shingle hiking its nails. The
boy is running, the duck on his head gyrating like a tin roof
half torn off, the bill drinking blood. The boy is running, his
mad hands flashing like a feather plucker in the belly down,

the duck cleated so the toe webs are stretched open and rubbery, adhering to the flesh below the hair. The boy is running for the farmhouse where his grandfather is at the gate jacking the manure from his boots, first one, then the other, so the sheep dung is there on the jack blade whickered with straw, and dark green, lincoln green, cud green, apple-shit green, a high sweet rose-garden stink instant and to be relished. The grandfather says nothing. With his eyes says, 'Don't hurt that duck boy.' Says, 'Ducks are money.' With his eyes. Turns. Walks towards the house. Leaves the boy with the duck on his head like a living hat.

Now try writing the smell of varnish, the taste of candy apple, the look of a compost heap, the feel of old leather...etc.

Exploring Simile

The following exercise begin as quite formulaic and move gradually beyond the formula. The simile (a comparison between two things using either the word 'like' or 'as) is a device which delights the reader and adds to the experience of reading. Similes are best when they are fresh, original and appropriate. Michael Ondaatje's poem, "Sweet Like a Crow" is a fine example of a piece of writing which is rich with fresh similes. The first exercise here is quite primary and a great deal of fun. The similes used therein are hyperbolic and meant to be playful and monstrous and appropriate to the spirit of the work.

Monster Poetry

The monster poem as practiced here begins at the head and moves to the toes. Each line contains a simile which is monstrous. The titles are playful and provide a counterpoint to the content.

My Sweet Valentine

My sweet valentine has a
head like a handful of squeezed margarine.
Hair like fish line tangled round a pike.
Eyes like two zeroes
on a dead butterfly.
Ears like telephones slammed on bubblegum.
Face like a pizza
thrown at an airplane propeller.
Skin like congealed white grease left in the frying pan
when it gets cold
after you've cooked bacon.
Shoulders like cactus
dropped upon a zebra.
Arms like snakes eight days in the road.
Belly like old tires
thrown on a bonfire.
Legs like nails hammered into cement.
Feet like the smell of tar on the wind.

*

My Aunt Tilldy's in Love with Egbert

Who has
hair like daisies in peat moss.
Head like a mouldy muskmelon
gone punk in a garden.
Eyes like red marbles bounced by thumbs.
Ears like gerbils attacked by barn cats.
Mouth like a glass of worms floating in white glue.
Chin like a cup of coffee jiggling on a tractor fender.
Shoulders like wooden teeth eating mashed potatoes.
Arms like gimp stretched between hound dogs.
Hands like Arthur Murray dance patterns
for the cha cha.
Fingernails like what you spit out
when you've chewed beyond the quick.

Legs like anacondas squeezing a pregnant Yak.
Feet like the wrong answer to
"Did the bomb drop on your house too?"
Or, "Whose head is that on the plate?"

My Boys' Smiles

My boys' smiles are
like ice cream's slow melt on the tongue.
Like cool water
    splashing over rocks in the distance.
Like the sound of the house
    when my wife is showering.
Like dogs in the hills
    at sundown.
Like waking to bacon smells at my grandmother's.
Like fire in a log
    on the coldest night of the year.
Like the stars
    in a black winter sky.
Like an egg's perfect oval
    in your palm.
Like setting a clock in a hotel room.
Like all day Saturday
    or the sound of car doors slamming
    when you expect company.

And you carry that feeling
with you all the way
through the week.
    *

    And finally, you might move well beyond the formula to compose a simile rich poem similar to that of Michael Ondaatje's "Sweet Like a Crow."

Because poetry...

With his poem, "Grid Erectile," Canadian poet Christopher Dewdney has inspired a new form of poetry each line of which begins with the word, "because" as in my own poem from my book, *The Pig Dance Dreams* (Black Moss Press, 1993).

On the Way Home From the Meat Factory
I Decided to Be a Poet

On the way home from the meat factory
I decided to be a poet!
Because sausages hung
like the long braids of Slavic girls.
Because the herd bull
took the worm of the bullet
in his skull
and fell like a dynasty.
Because the hogs
caught death on electric floors
and jittering were dragged still warm
in their fit's midst
to be halved like apricots
with their blue guts spilling
a circus-clown's nightmare on the floor.
Because their heads came severed
like hill fighters
for the deli.
Because the pure came oozing into plastic tubes
cinched and cut
cinched and cut in log-lengths of cold meat.
Because the cattle fell
like drunks in metal stocks
then were carbonadoed and hung to cure
in the time it takes
to light a cigarette in the wind.
Because blood spilled in the gutters

under the peeled beasts
and ran bubbling still hot
for the reservoir.
Because the chainsaws whined in bone
like a mosquito night
and the bandsaw cut clean portions
marbled with fat.
Because I hunger.
Because the hand that cuts the meat
feeds the city.
Because I hunger
and am human
on the way home from the meat factory
I decided to be a poet.

You might try writing a 'because' poem which is inspired by the causal or tight connection between action and event. The poem, "On the Way Home from the Meat Factory I Decided to Be a Poet" was inspired by a visit to an abattoir in Windsor, Ontario when I was seventeen. I grew up on a farm where we slaughtered our own animals for meat. I have very vivid recollections of hanging hogs in the apple tree. We also had a slaughter house on our property at what we referred to as 'the other place'. The village butcher used that slaughter house to do his killing. But nothing prepared me for the efficiency of the meat factory.

Exploring Metaphor

Metaphor is one of the most difficult of literary devices to master and yet it is also one of the most universal and important of devices. In its simplest terms, a metaphor is a comparison between two things in which the one thing becomes the other. It is used to establish connections between things. The best metaphors are those which are fresh, original and absolutely appropriate. The first of two exercises here, makes connections which are wild and dramatic and which require the author to make connections where there are none at first blush. The second exercise is more gentle and at first blush the reader hardly recognizes that the writing involves the creation of metaphor.

We Live on an Island Where...

Begin with the title "We Live on an Island Where ( ) Is/Are ( ) and fill in the parenthesis with a noun. Consider the following examples of titles generated by doing this exercise in schools across Canada.

We Live on an Island where Dragons are Hairspray

We Live on an Island where Heaven is Dolphins

We Live on an Island where Mom is Static Cling

We Live on an Island where Coconuts are Solid Gold Dancers

We Live on an Island where Garbage cans are Fashion Statements

We Live on an Island where Paradise is Peanut Butter

We Live on an Island where Dreams are Graffiti

We Live on an Island where Rainbows are Detectives

We Live on an Island where Shadows are Deja Vu

We Live on an Island where Taxis are Spatulas

*

We Live on an Island Where Shadows are Deja Vu

I have seen you
lying
like a grey cloak on grey sand.
You have waited for me
in ambergris tide pools
like dreams
of water in the distance.
You are a heartbeat
I have heard
under the sea.
You are
the fragrance of moonlight
in mist.
I have held you
like dust motes in sunbeams
remembered

The face of a child
is fading.
The green tresses
of a skull rock
wave
in submerged farewells.
I have seen the schools
of darting fishes
seeking your image
as smoke
seeks fire
in the rain.

*

We Live on an Island Where Dragons are Hairspray

My mom
has tiny stiff-winged dragons
in her hair
they flame
in her comb
like struck flints.
Her Sunday hat is fastened there
as a birthday cake
with a thousand tiny candles
flickering and breathing
blue fire like gas jets lit in midnight kitchens.
She thinks of baldness
as each follicle burns
like a tindered thatch of dry grass.
My mom
is hard to hug...
like hugging
the long lost ages
when damsels fell beneath the spell
of dragons
and they flew in her coiffure

like blue-green beauties
their wings on fire and flashing
above a summer pond.

Each of the titles above was generated by giving the students the opportunity to fill in the blanks and then as a group we decided upon what nouns to use. The challenge of the exercise is to write something in response to connections which are not obvious.

Riddle Writing

The object of all riddles is to tease the person solving the riddle with just enough information, but not too much information so that the person seeking to answer the riddle can succeed in getting the answer the author had in mind. The pleasure is available both in the process of seeking to answer the riddle and in achieving an answer which satisfies the riddle itself. In this exercise, the riddles are first and foremost poems. All the best riddles are in fact metaphors. They make connections which are not obvious.

Here is a riddle written by a child who had the child's stair-descending toy 'a slinky' in mind as an answer.

> *I am round*
> *I am silver.*
> *I go down the stairs*
> *very wild.*
> *What am I?*

The best answer I have ever heard for this riddle is not the one the author had in mind. The best answer, that is to say, the answer which has given the most pleasure over the years of my having used this riddle in classrooms is: 'your grandmother when the house is on fire.' This answer satisfies the riddle and it also has enough mischief in it to give a smile of pleasure to anyone who hears it.

Grandmothers are sometimes round especially if they are pleasantly plump. They can be silver if their hair is grey. The word silver is often used to describe grey hair. And your grandmother would certainly go down the stairs very wild if she were upstairs when the house was on fire.

And since it's a riddle we need not feel any of the peril or potential tragedy involved in a house fire. In the harmless context of the riddle the effect is purely comic.

In order to make a riddle which is also a poem, the creator must pay close attention to the poetics. The riddle might be quite short and simple or it might be long and complex. In order to be a good poem, the writer needs to pay close attention to the words. In order to write the poem as riddle, one might think of the object in mind and write towards it. What is wrong with each of the following as riddles?

> *I am round.*
> *What am I?*
> (not enough detail)

> *I am round.*
> *I am orange.*
> *I am a citrus fruit.*
> *I grow in California and Florida.*
> *You keep me in the fridge.*
> *I can be made into a pomander*
> *I can be made into juice.*
> *You sometimes take me to school in your lunch.*
> *What am I?*
> (too much detail)

Here is a simple riddle, though it's not much of a poem:

> *I live on a staple diet*
> *Though I am not alive.*
> *what am I?*
> (a stapler)

Here are a few riddles to consider as poems:

> *I can't be told.*
> *I'm seldom bold.*
> *I'm sometimes old.*

If you say me
I'm not me
any more.
What am I?
(a secret)

Outside
Inside.
Inside out.
Walk me outside.
What am I about?
(socks)

*

Who am I?

Of all the snowflakes in the sky,
Of all the sand upon the shore,
Of all the water in the sea,
Of all the starshine in the night,
Of all the dust within the blue,
Of all the people in the world,
Who am I?   (me)
And who are you?   (you)

*

I taste as water tastes
when it is pure.
I smell as a stone smells
in the centre of the stone.
I have the look of empty darkness
when there are no stars.
I am a stillness
without heartbeat
without breath.
Even in the deepest quiet
I am not there.

I am not there.
What am I?   (silence)

*

Believe me, don't believe me...
If you don't believe me
I am true as true can be.
If you do believe me
I am false as false is false...
what am I?   (a lie)

*

You can break me
though I'm never truly broken.
You can give me away
when words of love are spoken.
You can lose me
though I'm never truly lost.
You can give me freely
to a friend
and nothing is the cost.
what am I?   (the human heart)

When the Penguin Met the Polar Bear

When the **penguin** met
the **polar bear**
and the **tiger** met
the **king**.
the **cows** with **teeth**
on the **top** of their mouths
didn't say
a single thing...
The fisherman caught
himself a **whale**
for that
was the **fish** of his wish...

and the **spiders**
of the **insect** world
were feeling
cantankerish...
This cartoon of
our modern life
is quite enough
for some...
Well as for me
I find it sad
and terribly
troublesome...
Can you tell me why?

(penguins don't meet polar bears except in zoos because they are from
different poles. Penguins are from the far south and polar bears from the
far north. Cows have teeth only on the bottom jaw, not on the top. A
whale is a mammal, not a fish. Spiders are arachnids, not insects.)

Plainsong—the writing of imagist poetry

Imagist poetry in English dates back to around 1910. Poet Raymond
Knister was one of the first Canadian practitioners of this brief, laconic, Spartan style. He was influenced by the American poets who were
influenced by the French. F.S. Flint writing in 1913, set out the rules of
imagism as being:

1. Direct treatment of the "thing" whether subjective or objective.

2. To use absolutely no word that did not contribute to the presenta-
    tion.

3. As regarding rhythm: to compose in sequence of musical phrase,
    not in sequence of the metronome.

By this latter statement, in the words of Knister, the poet is
writing in 'plainsong.'

The famous oriental form of imagist poem is the haiku. The haiku is
a three line poem with five syllables in the first line, seven in the second and five in the third.

the lone shadow crawls
along deserted roadsides
also forgotten

Another verse form, 'the tanka' is five lines long. The first and third lines of the tanka are five syllables; the second, fourth and fifth lines are seven syllables.

Tanka on Faith

I breathe because I
believe in breathing, and I
have a kind of faith
in life. I hear my beating
heart: a closing rose...o p e n s

Excellence is very difficult to achieve in both of these forms. A favourite story of mine regarding the composition of the haiku goes as follows:

> Two great Shoguns were standing in the evening upon a field of battle each at the head of a great and perilous army. The one Shogun challenged his rival to the composing of a haiku. The two great warrior generals retired to their respective tents to write. The evening passed and so too the night. In the morning the two armies bristling in anticipation gathered to listen to their leaders' words. The armies were so impressed by the results that they retired from the battlefield and went home, satisfied that the power of a single poem had established the peace.

Re-read the poem by Margaret Saunder and review what is written about that poem in the essay, "Writing Poetry."

Through
    the autumn mist
a panting jogger

Consider the simplicity of expression, the economy of language, the compression of meaning, the use of the senses and the single image at the heart of the poem. Imagist poetry starts with an image. It is a still moment captured in tranquillity. And yet it does not limit itself to the visual. This remarkable piece of writing provides a brilliant example of how a simple seven word poem might excite the senses. As previously stated in the aforementioned essay, the reader feels the cool dampness and tastes the ozonation made available by the word mist. We also see the blinding white fog wall of the mist. We hear the 'panting.' And the use of the indefinite article introduces the jogger as 'stranger' and thereby suggests an ambient peril into the poem. A panting stranger whom the poet cannot see approaches through the fog. The shifting of the middle line to the right achieves movement in the poem. All this in seven words.

Read the following poems. Ask yourself what they have in common.

Returning to Night

We are returning
to night
where darkness comes
upon a nod of roses.

*

a leaf
withering down
falling smoke

*

my shoulder
in a sling
I carry a fish

*

A Fourteenth Way
for Wallace Stevens

the blackbird absent
his shadow
remains...

*

April rainfall
a sadness
on the glass

*

a siren
in the silence

*

fence posts
in a meadow
green earth greets the plough
*

bottle in the gutter
thirst
on its side

*

teeth of the lion
pride
in the grass
*

*

pale picket
fences
lazy old yards

*

and consider the power of a title...

Here is an imagist poem without a title:

the flower
in the mirror
smells of glass

The reflected image of the flower is not the flower. Neither is it a simulacrum since the real flower is implied by its presence. And yet, unlike the original, the image smells of the reflective surface and makes it immediately clear within the poem that the flower under consideration is not a flower, but a reflected flower. Not the real flower, but its reflected twin. Now consider the poem with its title, "the writer's dilemma".

the writer's dilemma

the flower
in the mirror
smells of glass

The title both clarifies and limits the meaning of the poem. The flower in the mirror is much like the flower in a poem in that it is distanced from the real flower by the artifice of recreation. The writer's dilemma involves the acceptance that experience transformed into language is always experience once removed. The use of language, however skillful, distances both the creator and the re-creator from the experience which inspired the work in the first place. The flower in the mirror is a reflected flower. The flower in a poem is a simulation of experience. A poem can never quite achieve its intention however much it may strive to be true to the experience which gave rise to it.

To quote Raymond Knister from his forward to *Windfalls for Cider*, "Birds and flowers and dreams are real as sweating men and swilling pigs. But the feeling about them is not always so real, any more, when it gets into words."

Considering Titles

Since imagist poems are so devoted to brevity, they often appear without titles. I have published the poem, "The Writer's dilemma" both with and without its title. I have come to prefer it with the title. Since poetry is often about the writing of poetry, most astute readers would get the point in any case. But I prefer to telegraph the meaning in this particular poem. That is not always the case. Margaret Saunders poem seems absolutely complete without the benefit of a title.

Writers should consider why poems have titles and when titles are appropriate. In my book, Stella's Journey, I removed all the titles from the poems since I wanted the poems to flow one into the next and for the book to read like a novel in verse. On the other hand when I published the poems originally and when I re-issued them as part of my selected poems I re-introduced the titles.

Titles serve several functions in poetry and prose. In addition to the obvious ease in identification, they function as either descriptive identifiers or as riddles for unlocking less obvious themes.

A famous example of the former is Blake's poem, The Tiger.

This title makes it immediately clear that at least on the surface the reader might expect to read a poem about a tiger. And when the reader considers the surface, the poem is indeed first and foremost about a tiger. There are of course deeper levels of the poem, but the title offers no hint of these deeper waters.

An example of the 'title as riddle' might be found in e e cummings poem, "Chansons Innocentes." Although this poem frequently appears without its title, it is my conviction that the title clearly unlocks levels of meaning missed by many readers.

The idea of this poem as a song of innocence unlocks the mystery of the metaphorical level of the poem. ' Of course the phrase 'songs of innocence' echoes Blake's poems "Songs of Innocence and Experience." The title requires a re-consideration of the poem.

I have taught this poem hundreds of times. As an exercise I give the poem to students in the absence of a title and ask them to give the poem a title. 90% of the respondents call the poem either, "Springtime," or

"Balloonman," or some variation on the two.

Confirmation that cummings himself sees the balloonman as a devil arises from the second poem in the series which repeats the refrain 'its the devil'.

Art inspired by Art

In the fall of 2000 I began working on a collaborative internet project with visual artist and photographer Marlene Menard. The project is called *The Yea Spot*. Marlene sends me each visual image via e mail. I write a poem in response to each of her pieces. Computer technology makes for ease in rapid communication of images and words. Marlene established a web site with each poem and corresponding image posted as hypertext on that interactive web site. This sort of ecphrasic work is but one example of a long-standing tradition of art inspired by art. The poem by Robert Browning, "My Last Duchess," is one of the most famous examples of poetry written in response to visual art.

At the University of Lethbridge in Lethbridge, Alberta, there is a metal sculpture which shapes the outline of a buffalo bull on the prairie horizon. Marlene took a photograph of that sculpture and I wrote the following poem inspired by both the original sculpture and the photograph of the sculpture.

The Invisible Buffalo

Somewhere the buffalo bull
supposes himself
as framing the sky to the shape of his shoulders
from the ghost-blue beauty
of a cloud-bellied wind
as if he were grazing on dream.
Somewhere he stands on a hill
in the mind
where grass waves away
and away

with a long farewell between friends
who in that disappearing distance
remember a lasting touch...
the thunder of hooves in the land
like the coming to life
of the hearts of the dead.

Poems can also be inspired by poems. As such they might be imitations of the original, such as parodies or homage. They might also simply be tributes to the original poem as in the poem, "So What is Not a
Question." This poem arises as a response to the news that the maple
tree which inspired popular Canadian poet Alexander Muir to write his
famous poem, "The Maple Leaf Forever." That poem was once so popular that it was memorized by every school child in Canada. And yet,
when the tree in Toronto was dying that fact was met by indifference on
the part of most Canadians including some young girls whom I asked
to write a poem in response to that event. They simply did not care. I
honoured their response by never using the story as an inspiration for
students again. And yet in Ireland songsmith Thomas Moore remains
popular and celebrated as does the great populist Scottish poet Robert
Burns. The last line of the poem refers to the fact that the original poem,
"The Maple Leaf Forever," was inspired by an autumn leaf that had
drifted from a particular tree onto Alexander Muir's sleeve.

So What is Not a Question

for Thomas Moore and Robert Burns

In Toronto at 62 Lang Street
when the old tree
which inspired Alexander Muir to write
The Maple Leaf Forever was dying circa 1999
a young girl told her summer teacher
"I can't write about
what I don't care about!"
And though committees were struck

to guy the brittlest branches for their girth
rigging ropes to windy places like a ship of sail...
it almost fell
despite the songbirds hopeless singing
flung to nothing in the fledgling's featherless chill
of each sparrow's broken-boned god
as by that ageless gravity they struck the earth unheard.
And though a throng of ghosts
might send their voices up
to thrill a thousand bowers
shivering last leaves
like the arboring hearts
of long-forgotten schoolroom children
what can I say, Ontario
—your car culture
can neither recall nor care for how one late-fall evening
long ago and gone
a large leaf drifted on a poet's sleeve...

Parody

A parody is a mocking imitation of an original work. Parody can be written in the spirit of the original or in a line by line mock imitation of the original. For example, try re-writing the great literary ballad, "The Highwayman" as a parody beginning thusly.

The Highwayman

The Robber of the Road

The Thief Who Steals from Travelers

The Bad Guy in a Mask Who Rides Late at Night and Robs Helpless Strangers

The wind was a torrent of darkness among the gusty trees

The zephyr was a lightless storm in the midst of the blowing woods

The breath of the world was a whirl of pitch within the windy arbor

The air current was a violence of lackluster in the middle of bend-

ing deciduous and coniferous plants

The moon was a ghostly galleon tossed upon cloudy seas,

The night-lit stone was a spectral barkentine bounced on overcast salt-water ways

<u>Diana was a phantasmagoric ship thrown upon murky bodies of water</u>

The satellite of midnight was a spooky boat hurled over cumulonimbus Mediterraneans

and so on...

The perfection of the original becomes immediately clear.

First Line Roulette

Another exercise in art inspired by art I call First Line Roulette. Try completing each of the following opening lines by using the line as the first line of a poem inspired by that line and then read the original. A variation on this technique is readily available to anyone with a book of poems, or even a book of short fiction. Flip open an anthology or poetry collection to any page at random. Simply copy out the first line of the poem without reading the poem in question. Complete the poem and then read the original. It is interesting to note as an aside that when I have used this technique in schools the results are strikingly like the original. If the original poem rhymes or has a regular rhythm, more often than not the imitations are similarly formal. And the content of the poems are often uncannily familiar. Elegies inspire poems about death. Dark moody poems result from poems with similar moods. Another variation on this exercise I call dictionary roulette. You simply open the dictionary at random, stab the page with your finger, write down the word you find there and begin a poem using that word. Or construct a poem by repeating the exercise.

Documentary poetry

The documentary poem is inspired by the life and times of an historical or legendary figure. It might also be a single poem inspired by a current event.

My book, *Tongues of the Children*, is a work of documentary poetry resulting from in-depth research into several little-known historical events such as: the Ancaster Assize of June 1814; the Duncombe Rebellion of 1837; the Irish famine and its resultant immigration; the underground railway and the Dawn settlement; and the Fenian invasion.

The poem "The Famous Execution of Timothy McVeigh" is an example of a poem inspired by a current event. You might sit down and read the newspaper and attempt a poem on a story of interest you find therein.

The Famous Execution of Timothy McVeigh

I have seen death
in the slow refusing of light
that comes with the expiring of cats
their eyes going dull as dragged glass.
I have watched
the awful blackness of sheep sight
in the pond-dark glance of their easing
a last exhale
like the dust from a hill in the wind
and been helpless
to feel their fear
for some say they have no soul.
If so, this is the end for them
of more than grazing.
This is more than the fading to grey of the hay in the barn
more than the flavour of oats gone stale.
This silence
is hopelessly pumiced
to a sharp divide
of a total emptying out
like seed bags slashed in a field
for the planter
under that spill to the drum
with the sandy sliding of time in the glass
drifting down.

I have watched my walking farmer father
casting out clover
in sweeps of his arm like the blowing sideways of rain
and there the broadcast future
falls and follows and catches the earth
where it clings to an almost greening
response in his wake—yet this killer
who died today
under the poison of state
with his heart like the rock of a stepped upon stone
going still
had no lasting words but these
looking round
"I am the captain of my soul"
and then the fatal burn
that brought the darkness came
and God
received him
as a woman might wave
an apron
at oven smoke
wondering what's ruined
what she might also
save.

June 11, 2001

Formal Verse

Formal verse is poetry which obeys the rules of rhyme and rhythm arising from certain genres of both lyric and narrative poetry. The literary
ballad for instance is often written in four line stanzas and obeys an (a
b c b / d e f e/ g h I h) scheme and so on. The meter of a literary ballad is as often as not the clip clop meter of the horse's hoof. This form
of poetry is not much used in the telling of modern stories since the
short story and snapshot fictions are preferred by most current story
tellers.

Formal verse fell out of fashion after the end of the first world war. It no longer seemed appropriate to express the thoughts and feelings of the poets of the time. Formal verse was largely abandoned by serious poets with a few notable exceptions. Its elegance and metronomic music became inappropriate to the predicament of modern humans coping with the death of colonialism and certain traditional values. Poems such as 'The Waste Land," and "The Love Song Of J. Alfred Prufrock" by T.S. Eliot set the standards for new writing. The free verse lyric has been the predominant mode of expression in modern poetry ever since.

As a young poet I began by imitating the masters of formal verse. I learned to write a sonnet before I learned to write in freer forms. I did this quite by accident, but I think it is an excellent way of learning to write poetry. I could rhyme naturally and employ meter long before I set myself free to imitate the free verse lyric.

However, a new formalism is emerging in contemporary poetry. And there are many examples of highly successful and beautifully appropriate formal verses in both modern and contemporary poetry. The following exercises provide examples of variations on the poetic forms such as the sonnet, the villanelle and the sestina.

The Sonnet

As previously stated, writing for me always arises out of a complementary connection between content, form and style. One of the main reasons why the sonnet has fallen out of fashion arises from the connection between its origins and its form. It became popular in English during the Renaissance as a means of expressing courtly love. The sonnet is perfect for this because its elegant rhymes reflect the formal relationship between men and women at a time when courting obeyed conventions of certain expected behaviours. Men were expected to woo their ladies in poetry. The iambic foot with its soft/hard soft/hard rhythms so resembles the sound of the human heart it seems intuitive and entirely correct that the sonnet would emerge as a poem of romantic love. In Canada the poets of the nineteenth century seemed quaint in part because they used the sonnet form in inappropriate ways to express their feelings about the Canadian landscape. Here are a few sonnets I have written with a rationale for the choice of the sonnet form.

Snow

The art of snow is in the winter air
And grieving white along dark branch's black.
The cold is resting like a leopard there.
It waits to fall upon a wind-flicked back.
And all the sky is full and ripe with pelt,
A blanket shook to fuzz a strife of light.
The softness lands and there begins to melt
Or freeze within those brittle arms of night.
The moon is lost and likewise are the stars.
The houses sit with candled window panes
And passing up the road, our moth-lit cars
While late night goers struggle up their lanes.
The smell of snow is like the smell of death.
Two lovers meet and die without a breath.

At the time of writing this poem, the sonnet form seemed perfect since I have always loved the snow and still dream of the first snowfall before it arrives. The closing couplet harkens back to the Elizabethan meaning for the word death which arises from the French petite morte or little death.

There are two sonnets in my book, *The Hockey Player Sonnets*. The sonnet seemed a perfect counterpoint to hockey and in the title poem, the sonnet here is either not a sonnet, or it is a sonnet with a bomb in the centre which makes it explode outwards against the chosen form. The Petrarchan or Italian Sonnet, "Where Will I Winter When I am Old" is love song dedicated to the game of hockey. The octave and sestet—argument and resolution of the form seemed absolutely appropriate to the idea of a man refusing to surrender to either aging or the long cold Canadian winters.

The Hockey Player Sonnets

for Al Purdy

1

What about them Leafs, eh!
(e.d.*) couldn't score an (e.d.) goal
if they propped the (e.d.'s) up
in front of the (e.d.) net
and put the (e.d.) puck on their (e.d.) stick
and the (e.d.) goalie fell asleep
and somebody (e.d.) yelled "SHOOT THE (e.d.) thing
(E-E-E-E. D-eeeeeeee!!!!!!!)

2

(e.d.) this (e.d.) shower's (e.d.) cold.
who the (e.d.) flushed the (e.d.) toilet?
give me the (e.d.) soap.
hand me that (e.d.) towel.
has anybody got some (e.d.) shampoo?
toss the (e.d.) over here!
thanks. what's this (e.d.) pansy (e.d.)?
who brought the (e.d.) beer?
toss me one. stop throwing that (e.d.) snow.
you could lose an (e.d.) eye.
and so on...

3

What do you mean you don't watch sports on TV.
Why the (e.d.) not?
Haven't you got an (e.d.) TV?
What the (e.d.) do you watch?
What the (e.d.) do you do?
Read!!!—who the (e.d.) wants to (e.d.) read!
too much like (e.d.) thinkin'.
there is much (e.d.) laughter at this.
and so it goes—
"what about them Leafs, eh..."

*expletive deleted

Where Will I Winter When I am Old

Oh where will I winter when I am old
And skates hang rusting in my outdoor shed?
Will my desire and my joy be dead
When all about the world is bleak and cold?
In muffled overcoat, galoshes rolled,
Slow-moving down the street with grey-haired head
While all my friends have either died or fled
Left me here grumbling, ever unconsoled.
A sun shines in the waiting summer south.
Of tan and coconut and ocean wet
They'll tell me I should quit my northern house.
Perhaps these wags will stop and leave me yet
To marvel at the river's frozen mouth
Where season tells what I cannot forget.

*

Again I returned to the sonnet form in the writing of my book, *Stella's Journey*, wherein I wrote two sonnets called the grandmother sonnets. It seemed absolutely appropriate because the poems were meant to be about the very traditional relationship between mother and subsequent generations. The subject of my long poem was my paternal grandmother Stella Lee nee Crosby. In this poem appearing early in the book, I use rural imagery combined with astronomical imagery inspired by her name 'Stella' which means star. I also wanted to capture the simple heartbeat of the child in the womb hearing the mother's heart.

Grandmother sonnets

I

Last night the moon was pale as painted stone
And like the lime-washed granite of a barn.
A man might build this month and stand alone
Beneath the stars of heaven hard to learn.
Among the many milk ghosts of the mind
The ditch remembers what the field has known

Where water runs ahead and leaves behind
The silt that steals its meaning from the loam.
And if by strength of will the field comes clear
I think of work that carries off the land
Whereon the frost might heave another year.
There is a stronger heart, a stronger hand.
A sister to the moon; a smaller tide—
The shadow of the blood she feels inside.

The Villanelle

Originally a French verse chiefly pastoral in content, the best example
of the villanelle in English is arguably Dylan Thomas' famous poem,
"Do Not Go Gentle Into That Good Night." A nineteen line poem comprised of five three line stanzas and a final four line verse, it employs
two rhymes aba aba aba aba aba and abaa. The opening line is repeated
in line 6, 12 and 18 and the third line is repeated in lines 9, 15, and 19.
Eight of the 19 lines thereby become a refrain.

I wrote the villanelle, "Old Bull's Villanelle" as part of my manuscript for the book, 'The Bad Philosophy of Good Cows." It was win-
nowed by the editor as unworthy of inclusion. I include it here as an
example of a failed experiment.

Old Bull's Villanelle

Old bull, you'd lie at rest upon your girth
When I was young and showing at the fairs
I'd doze down on your back and feel its worth.

Your legs tucked in; your belly on the earth
I'd chew on straw and free me of my cares.
Old bull, you'd lie at rest upon your girth.

When weary with the day you'd give me berth
And breathing warm, I'd feel what feeling shares.
I'd doze down on your back and feel its worth.

When kindness least is kindness, most is dirth
Then boy gives in to diffidence and stares.
Old bull, you'd lie at rest upon your girth.

I value most what you are bringing forth.
The loneliness that being lonely bares.
I'd doze down on you back and feel its worth.

And smiling in my way, a quiet mirth
I'd wear the sort of love a lover wears.
Old bull, you'd lie at rest upon your girth.
I'd doze down on your back and feel its worth.

Triolet

The triolet is a simpler French verse. It consists of eight lines. First two
lines are repeated as the last two lines, the first recurring as the fourth.
The rhyme scheme is abaaabab

The White Cow Triolet

Oh, my sister walked so long ago
With a heifer wild and white.
Haltered and trained, she walked her slow.
Yes my sister walked so long ago
With that heifer white as a field of snow
She was young and handsome, quite
When my sister walked so long ago
With a heifer wild and white.

Sestina

Often described as one of the most difficult and complex of various
French forms of poetry, the sestina is a poem consisting of six six-line
stanzas and a three-line conclusion. Note the end words of the first six
lines of the first stanza. The last word in the second stanza is a repeti-
tion of the last word in the first, the last word of the second line in the
second stanza is the same as the last word in the first line of the first
and so on as in: (1, 2,3,4,5,6—6,1,2,3,4,5—5,6,1,2,3,4—4,5,6,1,2,3
and so on.)

The poem, "Sestina on a Cattle Truck," appeared in the book, *The Bad Philosophy of Good Cows.*

Sestina on a Cattle Truck

for Al Purdy

Riding in the back of a transport truck
With all the sheep and jostling tethered cattle
Where cigar-mouthing half-mad Blake,
Leaning into high-piled hay and rattled pails
Stood to mumble out a poem he'd been reciting
About a gopher in a pasture just as green

As the breath of well-chewed hay is green.
And so we rode the highway in that truck,
The metal sheeting shivering over the cattle
And over the words half-heard from Blake
His hand resting on the bottom of a water pail.
Yet though he'd drowned in noise, he stood reciting.

What he'd learned as a child he was reciting
Now remembered as it were when he was green.
In the back of Rankin's transport truck.
And Dan McGrew, though ghostly, bothered not the cattle
Bathed in motion, they suffered not from Blake
Who thumped a steady rhythm on the upturned pail

Though the sheep were worried by his fist upon that pail.
They joggled at the gate for his reciting.
Ignored the hay though it were inviting green
And flocked into the corners of the truck.
But this was no concern to the tied-up cattle
Who sniffed the passing road ignoring Blake.

And on he went, this barded Blake
His words as hollow as if hallooed in a pail.

I know no now, nor knew then, why he kept reciting
The words he'd caught in air amongst the passing green
That took the silver we could see beyond the truck
And wind-sniffed highway moving underneath the cattle.

Yes, and groomed for show they were, those cattle.
Groomed more finely than this sweating Blake
Who spat a final muggy stub into a water pail
As if it were a word not worth reciting
And mumbled out a line spit over-green
Inside the silence within the stopping truck.

Then open came the door on his reciting
From half-light must onto the waiting green
We tumbled down the ramp and off that truck...
    off that awful cattle truck.

The Ode

The modern ode is a poem of high praise comprised of several ten-line
stanzas.

Ode on a St. George Street Crow

You sit like a fat dollop
of dropped tar
on the high slender branch drooping
above the neighbourhood this morning
your feathers
like the bristles of a roofing brush
fibered with rain
from balmy skies
that drift with dissipating rivers of mist
carded like burr's wool where you take your watch.

You look, I suppose
for the road-kill squirrel,

the carrion coon,
the luckless cat who flashed his eyes
one final time like green glass lit from behind.
And if you find a rancid bit of flesh,
a gluey swatch of fur,
you might detach and come and bend above the meat
like a small black umbrella
broken in a cross-fall wind.

You open your throat and caw
like a hinge on an attic door
unoiled for fifty years.
A vintage cry
under heaven's old shadows.
the priest of wet weather
you shake your cassock an d
briefly rending your vestments for lice
you smooth again and like a licorice bottle
flow into a lightless perfect mass of self.

Do you remember the corn rustling
like stiff Victorian women serving tea?
How you lit in murders
of ten jet-black rags
and robbed the crop
like broken jewellery counters
careless of the cobs and kernels
that spilled their bounty
then you loaded the empty field-side tree
like frozen fruit that never dropped.

When I hear the wind's geriatric
breathing in the pine
like an accordion
wheezing open on one hand
and I look up to see you

in the thick of needles
swaying like a drunkard's top hat
and happy with the world
I wish you well and bless your purpose
keeping time in the great green metronome of conifer.

And then you pluck and fly
like a branch of half-burned leaves
and take your station
in the maple wood
creaking like a set of village hardwood stairs
and plump as widow's knitting—
the only life for seven trees
like Rimbaud's opium wombed in smoke
the fog that frames a dream
with a warm and living core.

And here I walk beside the road
the colour of school-room slate
late in the day after the janitor has come
in the rain-wet smell of early winter
by the trees girdled in bark
where you regard the street
look to the festered lamb leg
of red berries in the frosted bush
and dream of blood above the flesh
the cut that makes a brotherhood of predator and prey.

I celebrate you, inky crow
who like a throb of oil
convulsing to keep suspended
in the precise dynamic of your birdness
flux and fold in a weird
encompassment of light
pulsing like a black dissolve
flexing wings in the come and go
an Edwardian gentleman's

metamorphosis of cape and cane.

I celebrate you, inky crow
who like a velvet bull
is black whichever way he's brushed
and king of shivers
cacophonous as stubborn colds
you rule the perch of morning till evening
like a tailor's scrap
fluttering from the scissors to the floor
and to our matador of roses
we give true hearts away.

The Elegy

The elegy is a poem which pays tribute to the dead.

My Old Dog Died in My Arms

I felt him go loose
and he slid
from the sweet domestic circle
of my embrace forever
his eyes
empty as pools of tea-brown ink
and I could hear a suffering October window
grieving rain
as if it cared
I sensed him slacking
and was surprised by how light and frail he seemed
how like a balsa thing
weary as a slanting cone of dry beach sand
drifting into a hollow
ribbed with sticks
he slipped
and was no more
I will bear the burden of my kindness

at the end
and find it hard
to love this dreary world
this morning
weeping, this October mourning
when my heart weighs broken
like the thread that kept these water droplets
from tracing gravity to its source
in the glass.

Found Poems

A found poem is a poem arising from text already written. Since I write a fair amount of documentary poetry and creative non-fiction poetry, and in so doing am engaged in a great deal of research, I have employed found text transformed into poetry quite often.

This first example is taken from court documents taken from the Ancaster Assize of 1814.

Having been found guilty
of the crime of High Treason
you are to be taken to the place from whence you came
and from there to be drawn on hurdles
to the place of execution
where you are to be hanged by the neck
but not until you are dead
for you must be cut down alive
and your entrails taken out
and burnt before your faces
(and your being still alive)
then your heads to be cut off
and your bodies divided
into four quarters
and your heads and quarters
to be at the King's disposal.
And God have mercy on your souls.

These being the words of Chief Justice
Thomas Scott
pronouncing sentence
at the Court of Oyster, Ancaster, Ontario
on Tuesday, June 21, in the year of our Lord, 1814.

*(*this was the only occasion of such sentence being pronounced and
eventually carried out on North American soil, and the last instance of
its ever being declared in the Commonwealth)*

Why They Were Whipped

one young slave girl was whipped
because she called
her mammy "mother"
which was considered
too near the white way
another said
"my father was whipped
because he looked
at a slave they'd killed,
and wept"
a black child
was whipped
for playing with a white girl's doll
a hungry boy
was whipped
for eating a biscuit
a woman
was kicked and struck
so she had to crawl away
for begging her new master
to buy her baby
as well
one man was severely whipped
for saying aloud his real name

which was William
an attractive young woman
was whipped by her master, known for kindness,
when she protested her rape
by an overseer
black drivers
were whipped
for failing to flog field hands
a good husband,
for defending his wife
against beating
was battered about his bloodied head
whipped till his back
was lacerated with welts
and open wounds
and then was suffered
to have his right ear cut off
meanwhile
is it any wonder
the cook playing dumb in the kitchen
should spit in the biscuits
and pee in the coffee
meant for the white folks in the big house
with their bullwhip
like a Chinese giant's black moustache
hanging loose from the wall of the barn.

This poem ends with original lines, but uses text taken directly from history and changed only here and there to enhance the literary effect.

The poem, "The Legend of the Peaches," taken from my book, "Soldier's Heart," is inspired by a true story and employs lines taken directly from the text remaining true to the original text only in the opening stanza.

The last verse of the poem is invention based upon what is suggested by the story as taken from history.

The Legend of Peaches

It was Christmas week
and the boys marched along
at the stream Brankhorst Spruit
36 miles short of Pretoria
with the lads in a jaunty mood
eating peaches
and listening to the strains
of the regimental band playing
"Kiss me mother/
kiss your darling daughter"
and singing the smell of fruit
when the rebel Boers
opened fire
and before the British could break their lines
there were so many killed
in the withering
that a century could not name the dead
at one a year
and the bandsmen lay at their bugles
breathing blood
as their last breath struck heaven
in a single groan
like the dying drone
of the pipes
their rifles still cold in the wagon
stiff as the tossed-down stalks of harvest.
And so the soldiers were buried where they died
and legend has it
that the peaches in their pockets
burst open and
grew into a grisly line
of trees.
And this is the fruit of the grave
taking root

at the hip of the dead
or in the skull of the man
with the stone in his mouth
and the touch of his face in the earth
like the flesh of a peach
and the taste of his soul
still sweet.

Where Poetry and Prose Meet

Referred to variously as prose poetry, the lyric paragraph, snapshot fiction, postcard fiction, or as one anthologist called it sniglets the short lyrical prose work occupies the common ground between poetry and prose. The more musical and descriptive the voice, the more likely it will be referred to as a prose poem. The more narrative, the closer to the fictive voice, the more likely it will be referred to as fiction. What makes it appropriate to call it prose is the fact that the writing is organized in sentences and paragraphs rather than being broken into lines and stanzas. Analyze the work and ask yourself as a reader whether the work is in the singing voice, or the telling voice or the saying voice. The label is only helpful if it assists you in the writing of the thing. The movement of time, the occurrence of event, the rhythms of the moment or series of moments which give rise to story, these are the important considerations. The one common truth of all the following pieces is that they are compressed and compelled by the need to write the thing in as few words as possible. The prose poem or snapshot fiction is generally between two-hundred and seven hundred words.

Each of the following sentences is the first sentence in either a prose poem or a piece of snapshot fiction. Use the sentence as an opening sentence in your own writing and then read the original work that follows.

1. More than forty years a ghost, I've faded now, the very substance of my specter gone like snow landed on warm ground.

2. Teacher crossed the room with purpose, her heels fastening nails down deep in the floor like a barn being built in the distance.

3. When the men come in from thrashing there is the wet hubbub of washing in the outdoor tub.

4. Today, this very morning, we killed Bob Dick and stole his horses.

5. Things are more terrible at home than you can imagine.

6. from bandy legs to beer legs

7. I want to be the poet of your kneecaps.

1. More than forty years a ghost, I've faded now, the very substance of my specter gone like snow landed on warm ground. But I too was born once. Born at home, like most. While the small mad calliope of the kitchen kettle shrilled on the iron stove, I came caterwauling into the world on a fine day, the ninth of June, 1885. My mother fair, though temporarily occupied; my father handsome and well-healed, handing out cigars. I flopped into the doctor's hands like greased dough. Cut loose, I sucked at life. The warm milk of mother Mara in my mouth sweet. I would live seventy years. I would die in bed in a city fifty miles from home. My husband's words for that passing, "Is she gone then?" Surely my life had purpose. Consider then my hours on the earth and the great darkness before and after.

   My name Stella, means star. I rose in that ancient heaven and shone for twenty-some thousand days until the autumn solstice fell upon the farmhouse, and I twinkled out like a sinking spark.

   from *Stella's Journey*

2. **The Strapping**

   Teacher crossed the room with purpose, her heels fastening nails down deep in the floor like a barn being built in the distance. I straightened up. Froze in place. Teacher reached her desk swimming the thick black-strap silence. Her desk drawer slid open. I walked towards her crooked finger. I saw the strap she held hanging down like a tail. Teacher took my palm, turned the lifeline to the light, straightened the fingers, and began the windmill sweep of heat and flame. Teacher. Adult teacher, rocked back on her heels and whistled leather. The hard thing snapped into flesh. Stung and stung again my little hand. My mouth quivered and went wet. I knew now what she meant when she'd said, "do what I say." My game had come to this. Five, I think. Five times she struck. At each blow I shuddered and winced and shut my eyes for fear. Five. Never again would I do anything wrong. Never again, I promised. Only moments before we had all been laughing. Now the room was quiet. Only the cruel children were glad of this event. Never again would I ever, ever do anything wrong. And I was six years old. And she was fifty. And never again would I ever do anything wrong. I promise. I promise. My hot hand. I promise never to play the bull again. I'll sit very still and be a good boy. I'll never laugh out loud or play the bull again. I promise. I promise. My little six year old hand hot as tea service. My little red six year old hand.

The very next day, Dick Lowell and I took the strap out of teacher's desk and pretended the squeers. Of course we were caught. And Dick's hand was like old paint before the end of the year. And I remember and refuse to forgive.

from *Stella's Journey*

3. **The Men**

When the men come in from thrashing there is the wet hubbub of washing in the outdoor tub. Their golden forearms, their grit-rimmed napes, the knob of their spines articulated like old hickory. They talk gaily of the golden blast that knocked the tiny hired man mowing backwards in a thick wind. And the laughter as he comes houseward after like a scarecrow come to life half-stuffed. And he washes last leaving the water black and murk and well-strawed.

And they come in through the kitchen for the middle room. Doffing their caps where the table is heavy with harvest in the cool dark centre of the house. And they do not mind the work of women. They expect busy daughters and rapid invisible wives. The platter of beef floats by in a circle rushed light with hunger. The potatoes pass from clouds into a blink at the bottom of the bowl. The vegetables reconfigure in smaller portions. The bread shrinks on the loaf. The butter melts back in a yellow retreat like heated gold. And of a sudden the seconds come. The pattern dresses fly about in happy servitude working the crowd of bellies, working the thirsty crew. And the men lean back. Loosen their posture notch by notch. Apple down the length of themselves to the laces. Lean back and pick their teeth. And lick the syrup from their spoons.

One fellow pulls a fieldmouse peeping from his pocket. Dips him like a candle wick in the maple syrup at the table centre. The rodent goes hip and shoulder sinking in the super-sweet darkness. And the prankster tips back his head, lowers the wet mouse in his own wide mouth, and pulls him out clean. He mumbles laughter looking to the women for the shock of it.

But Stella hides her disgust. Clears the table in sour silence. Begins the afterdance in the happy absence of men. Gathers back the ruin. Pours away what's left of the syrup like the unwatched passing of afternoon light.

from *Stella's Journey*

4.   This Morning We Killed a Man, and this is How it Happened

Today, this very morning, we killed Bob Dick and stole his horses. Damn good horses too. They was almost worth it. We come up the lake shore walkin' on the sand. It was about a mile from pa's old place and the sand was froze a little, which was quite strange for this early in the fall. Bob was still in bed so we was just going to take his horses and skedaddle. Trouble was Bob's hired man Jake Tooney was waitin' there with a loaded gun like he was expectin' us. I ain't absolutely too sure, but somebody must have tipped him to the fact that we was comin'. He didn't say nothin'. Just shot Tommy Martin in the ear. How a man can manage to make any kind of sound when his brains is hove in I don't know, but Tommy fell crowin' and whistlin' like a bird in a snake fight.

crowin' and whistlin' like a bird in a snake fight.

None of us knew he was dead till Jimmy Hyde screamed, "J-j-j-jesus H. C-c-c-christ. T-t-t-tommy's d-d-d-dead." And then we all seen the blood come leakin' out from under his head like rum from a busted rum jug.

Jake Tooney run in the house and we made quick for cover except John Dickson who never seemed afraid of nothin'. He just walked over to the barn, unlatched the door and in five minutes come out with them two fine geldings of Bob Dick's bridled and ready to go.

We was all layin' low as dogs in the shade when Bob come racketing out onto the porch.

"You lead them horses back where you got them, Mister."

John Dickson just smiled. He has a way of smilin' that says the same as when other men spit. I could see pa out of the corner of my eye. He was lyin' very still, taking a bead on Robert Dick. It reminded me of how still pa could be when he wanted to be. I'm pretty certain pa was waitin' for some sign that Robert Dick was worth killin' when somebody else shot him right on the word Mr.. Anyways, whoever it was made a mess of his face. He crashed back into the door and gargled blood for a whole minute before he expired. John Dickson never stopped smilin'. He just turned around and walked away like he'd trick-traded for them horses. Pa eased the hammer of his piece and stutterin' Jimmy Hyde he whimpered like he was a dog locked in a gutting shed.

We buried both corpses in the same grave. It looked a little like they was huddled together to keep out the cold. Funny thing about that business. They never tried any of us for the murder of Robert Dick. And both of them horses died from pneumonia. And I heard how Jake Tooney fell in the creek and drowned. When they found him he had a fish hook in both his eyes. My guess is, he must have been usin' the wrong kind of bait.

from *Tongues of the Children*

5.   a letter home

dear john

things are more terrible at home than you can imagine. I weep to write these words and glory in the fact that we have got away and would that I had never returned, for surely, I will be haunted all my days by the spectre of those good people we left behind us here in Skibbereen. it is a town you would not recognise, though it was once our own. since you have asked after the health of a few kith and kin of the county, I will endeavour to tell you some of what I have found, but that it shall not disturb your sleep as mine own has been ruined, let me say simply that it is the luck of the ghosts to be gone for I bear witness to the fact that the living suffer beyond hope and wish themselves away with their God as well.

the streets of the hamlet are deserted and there's not enough bread in the country to save a poor priest his church's mouse. I entered Maggie Cross's cottage as we had done so often together before we sailed. I swear I found neither her, nor her little son Sean, nor Nora, nor Johnny O", nor her sister, nor her niece. I found in their stead five souls and a corpse so small in their bones I wish the earth had fixed them a better more eternal rest. the living did not rise from their cots for they were so sick with starving they might as well have been made from moonlight as made from flesh. I will not perfume their awful passing with further description. there's no poetry so sad it might say what I have seen. And Paddy O'Drake is gone as is his wife and little girl. And so it is with George Hill, your good friend and mine. And all the estate I see is that of the grave. and the women lie half naked in nothing but a barley cloth or ragged blanket that does no earthly good but to hide a little of what it was to call themselves, themselves.

I saw a man half eaten by rats that dragged his hand across the street to share the fingers. I cannot say more. my pen falters to put it down. there is here a tide of death too high to shore against. I fear I shall go mad for my brain is injured with grief and my heart is broken. keep away John. the hundred are dead in the thousands. I am leaving. there is nothing to do. the man you knew, you shall not see again and the man you see again when he returns shall not be he as he was. ask not after your father, nor his dear wife, your mother. all Ireland's a fevered ghost. All help for them that's there is gone.

your friend

g.g.

from *Tongues of the Children*

6   from bandy legs to beer legs

from kids hacking it out between snow boot goals on ponds, gravel pits, frozen creeks and backyard and schoolyard rinks

to old timers grinding it out in pickup games in the late night arenas of little towns and big cities all across the country and for all the glory between

for the players with plenty of heart and soft hands

for the pylons and hackers who keep going though they have nothing to give but their love of the game

for the fathers and mothers up by five and out by six on the coldest morning of the winter

for their sons and daughters—

from wobble skaters with their kitchen chairs to showboats and sharpshooters

for the netminders, for the blueliners, the centres and wings

for the spectators who watch and for the players who play

for what we remember and what we dream

this is hockey

–introduction to the anthology of hockey writing *That Sign of Perfection*

7. And here is a piece as it appeared as both a poem and a piece of prose used to introduce an anthology of the same title.

I Want to Be the Poet of Your Kneecaps

I want to be a poet
of your kneecaps
to call them out
like an archaeologist
gently brushing earth from a curve
of painted crockery
a thousand year old preciousness
he might hold in his palm
saying, this is the reason I am
alive, I exist to rescue
the ages residing at your bending legs.
I want to be the poet
of your ankles
those rosebuds closed above your feet
on either side
to say
there is a promise blooming
in the bone
a sweetheart's secret pressed forever
in that book of flesh.
I would be
the poet of the nape of your neck.
I would be the poet
of toes.
I would linger
musing on the neat fiveness
of your hands
the tiny divot of your philtrum
the creases of your ears.
Surely the blueness of your iris
is pool enough for some,
but what of the pupil
black as a circle of felt
on a false poppy.
Yes, there are certain obvious
flowers of longing
but I would be the poet

of difficult desire
let me celebrate
the slight plumpness of the belly
about the navel
let me be the words connecting your luminous cable
to the stars.

from *Never Hand Me Anything if I am Walking or Standing*

I want to be a poet of your kneecaps to call them out like an archaeologist gently brushing earth from a curve of painted crockery a thousand year old preciousness he might hold in his palm saying, this is the reason I am alive, I exist to rescue the ages residing at your bending legs.

I want to be the poet of your ankles those rosebuds closed above your feet on either side to say there is a promise blooming in the bone a sweetheart's secret pressed forever in that book of flesh.

I would be the poet of the nape of your neck. I would be the poet of toes. I would linger musing on the neat fiveness of your hands, the tiny divot of your philtrum, the creases of your ears.

Surely the blueness of your iris is pool enough for some, but what of the pupil black as a circle of felt
on a false poppy.

Yes, there are certain obvious flowers of longing, but I would be the poet of difficult desire.

Let me celebrate the slight plumpness of the belly about the navel. Let me be the words
connecting your luminous cable to the stars.

from the introduction to the anthology *I Want to Be the Poet of Your Kneecaps*

Writing Fiction

The voices in fiction writing can be divided into the four modes. These are the descriptive, the narrative, the dramatic and the expository. The descriptive voice freezes the moment and concentrates its attention upon the image. It might be said to be the singing voice. At its best the descriptive voice shares a vivid lyricism with the poetic. The narrative voice adheres to the rhythms of time, though it need not do so slavishly. Events occur as things unfolding in the present. They might also occur as recollections from the past or as imagined in a fictive future. The explorations of events in time need not occur chronologically, nor do they need to be true to real time. Time might leap back and forward in service of the telling voice. The dramatic voice might also be referred to as the 'saying' voice. In fiction the dramatic voice is employed in the creation of dialogue. As stated in the previous chapter on writing fiction, this voice is the most slavishly true to real time. Characters say their words in the same time as it would take them to speak if they were real people. The expository voice is the voice which informs the reader. This voice is the most artificial in service of fiction.

An exercise in writing description

Read the two pieces of writing and then write a piece of your own involving being 'somewhere in the morning.' Pay special attention to the masterful way in which Hemmingway writes description without reliance upon adjectives. And remember to engage the five senses in writing description.

Somewhere In the Morning

Almost every morning you will find him at his desk. He is alone. The room is silent save one solitary faux school clock sounding the wall with the wag of its pendulum. The air around him is redolent with the perfume of books, some, their pages brown, seem to crack like burning paper. He is alone in the house. The furnace booms once in the basement. There is a rush of blue fire he cannot see circling the jets in the heart of his home. No one comes to his door. No one phones. No one enters. He is breathing in and diving deep.

The coffee goes cold in his cup. It tastes of yesterday. It tastes of bitter promises. He remembers everything. The writing goes well. The snow begins its soft applause upon the study glass. He closes the door. Leaves. He is alone.

*

You know how it is there in the morning in Havana with the bums still asleep against the walls of the buildings; before even the ice wagons come by with ice for the bars? Well, we came across the square from the dock to the Pearl of San Francisco Cafe to get coffee and there was only one beggar awake in the square and he was getting a drink out of the fountain. But when we got inside the cafe and sat down, there were the three of them waiting.
–opening paragraph from Earnest Hemmingway's novel *To Have and Have Not*

Poet James Reaney says of writing, 'if you can't write a description of your verandah, then you can't write.' Further to this he adds that we should know the name of everything from our front doorstep to the sidewalk.

Give yourself a test. Glance out the window of your dwelling and see how many things you can and cannot name. Make an inventory of these and make it your business to find out the names of the things with which you are familiar and which you cannot name.

Write a description of your balcony, your front porch, your back deck, the entryway of your building...etc. Write a description of your own bedroom. As W.O. Mitchell says, 'write the smell of varnish."

Read the following passage by Brian Moore taken from his novel, Judith Hearne, and attempt a drawing of the room he is describing. Take note of lovely and masterful connection between the protagonists mood and the ambient description of the room. It is very quickly clear that the predominant mood is one of loneliness and alienation.

She sat up, her hair falling around her shoulders, feeling a gelid draught through the flannel stuff of her nightgown. Her thighs and calves, warmed in the moist snuggle of sheets were still lax, weary, asleep. The gilded face of her little travelling clock said ten past seven. She lay back, pulling the yellow blankets up to her chin, and looked at the room.

A chair, broadbeamed, straightback, sat in the alcove by the bay window, an old pensioner staring out at the street. Near the bed, a dressing table made familiar by her bottle of cologne, her combs and brushes, and her little round box of rouge. Across the worn carpet was a wardrobe of brown varnished wood with a long panel mirror set in its door. She looked in the mirror and saw the end of her bed, the small commotion of her feet ruffling the smooth tucked blankets. The wardrobe was ornamented with whorls and loops and on either side of the door mirror was a circle of light-coloured wood. The circles seemed to her like eyes, mournful wooden eyes on either side of the reflecting mirror nose. She looked away from those eyes to the white marble mantelpiece, cracked down one support, with its brass fender of Arabic design. Her Aunt D'Arcy (a photograph) said good day in silver and sepia-toned arrogance from the exact centre of this arrangement, while beside the gas fire a sagging, green-covered armchair awaits its human burden. The carpet below the mantelpiece was worn to brown fiber threads. She hurried on, passing over the small wash basin, the bed table with its green lamp, to reach the reassurance of her two big trunks, black-topped, brassbound, ready to travel.

She twisted around and unhooked the heavy wool dressing gown from the bedpost. Put it on her shoulders and slid her feet out of bed into blue, fleecy slippers. Cold, a cold room. she went quickly to the gas fire and turned it on, hearing its startled plop as the match poked it into life. She spread her underthings to warm; then fled back across the worn carpet to bed. Fifteen minutes, she said, it will take fifteen minutes to heat the place at all.

Here is an example of my own writing about the farmhouse and childhood there.

I love the way the world works. The way a June morning can hoist its flag of wild current smells over the yard owning every molecule form here to star life and back. How it wakes with birdsong that lifts the silence from the grass like a fragile kite and how light soaks through the branches like amber wine. How the slow and solitary voice of a milk cow can drift across the pasture like a coffee smell. I love the clack of a wooden screen door letting children out and in through fly buzz and the slanting hubbub of breakfast sounds. How the morning talk across a table can make or break a day, the life till then like a puzzle finished and carried across a level room. The way the space between souls closes just a little then within the safe circle of hearts alike, we almost believe we'll surely improve the days to come.

from *The Art of Walking Backwards*

*

We played a game of hiding from our friends on the edge of gardens lying among the apple stain and tall grass under porches draped in webs that clung to our faces like an old maid's bridal veils. We hid beneath beds breathing in the wool tags of dust deep in barn mows smelling of bird lime in the hay. We hid between corn rows rustling like jewelry-shop tea cups packed in blue boxes. We incubated in cars, pined in closed closets, knelt in fruit cellars where glass-jar peaches floated and bumped together like the moons a fish might dream. And we were feeling the delicate thrill of spies watching through knothole cameras, seeing the calves of cousins walk by disembodied by bedskirts. We listened with our ears to the door for the safe conspiracies coming close almost always betrayed by our own deep and secret desire to be found, with not one Anne Frank among us to die, her heart throbbing in the game when jackboots take the stairs.

from *Never Hand Me Anything if I am Walking or Standing*

An exercise in writing narration

The narrative or 'telling voice' requires that we discover what stories there are within us to tell. As for me, I discovered that I had a great deal to write about the farm on which I was born and raised. It wasn't until I had written several other books that I began to go back to my roots and mine my childhood. The first book in which I did this was my book, Hired Hands. Since then I have observed certain recurring motifs in my work. One of them is a concern with ground wells. The other involves a recurring interest in autobiographically important trees. Return to the chapter on writing fiction and review and explore the exercise 'dragging a tree through your life.'

What if?

Ideas for fiction writing can often be generated by the creation of 'what if's.' Consider each of the following and generate three ideas of your own in each genre and then attempt a piece of fiction arising from one of the ideas.

Realism

- What if you'd stolen a chocolate bar from a local store and the phone rang?
- What if you'd been attacked by bullies and they'd taken your birthday gift Starter Jacket?
- What if the teacher came to the door to talk to your parents?

Fantasy

- What if you couldn't wake up and every dream you dreamed came true?
- What if you went to sleep in your own bed and woke up in Madrid in a bull ring?
- What if you were in a television set being watched by your parents and you couldn't get out?

Science Fiction

- What if you opened your window and saw the red earth of Mars just beyond the garden?

- What if you noticed that your mother had a tail and your father had wires in the back of his head?

- What if every time you looked in the mirror whatever you saw came alive and entered the room, including your own double?

Mystery

- What if you had been hypnotized to kill the next person to enter the room?

- What if your mother were living a second identity and her first life came back to haunt her?

- What if you began to poison your neighbours' pets?

Romance

- What if you had two girlfriends/boyfriends and they were both coming to dinner?

- What if this were your wedding day, and you didn't want to get married?

- What if you met someone who promised to take you away to live in South Africa and this was your last day at home?

Melodrama

- What if you were a mad scientist and changed brains with your sister?

- What if the landlord were kicking your family out of their house today?

- What if Count Dracula came to dinner?

Ghost Story

- What if you were the only person in the room who isn't dead?

- What if you were dead and didn't know it?

- What if the butcher knives began to move toward your hand, blade out?

Adventure and/or War story

- What if you were on a house boat in the Amazon?
- What if it were July 1st, summer of 1863 outside Gettysburg, Pennsylvania?
- What if you were on an airplane about to land in Alaska?

Suspense

- What if you heard the sound of ticking and you knew it was a bomb?
- What if your girlfriend/boyfriend were hiding in the pantry?
- What if you were in a time machine without a time control knob so you never knew where you would arrive?

Fable

- What if your dog could talk?
- What if you were a cat?
- What if the butter spoke to the toast?

An exercise in writing conversation

The writing of conversation requires that we develop listening skills. The best way to write effective dialogue in fiction is to begin by listening well. Characters speak differently. They speak according to their personality, their education, their mood, their geography, and they also modify their speech to fit the environment in which they are conversing and to the object of their conversation.

Write 'a dinner table conversation,' and then read the following example.

The Conversation

Once upon a farm there were two elderly brothers who never spoke. Or rather, it was not so much that they never spoke, but that they never spoke to each other, though they'd lived in the same house, on the same farm, at the same time all their lives. The elder brother was a bachelor; the younger a married man. One was an uncle; the other a father. The uncle had a nephew. The father had a son. The son had a sister. The sister had a mother. The mother had a father-in-law. And, the father-in-law, a widower by then, whose wife Stella had died, had a hired man. And they all lived together in the same house. The lucky seven.

Each morning at breakfast they came to the table in their own good time. Every day the hired man crept down the stairs into the dark, gas-lit kitchen, and prepared himself to eat alone by the light of that blue flame. He sat in the quiet at the table spreading his morning meal before him. Eating heartily for one warm hour. After he was done, he went for the barn for his morning constitutional in the cow gutter. And he always stole two pieces of white bread for his blonde collie dog, Tippy. And then he smocked his way across the cattle yard busy with his chores. Watering the cattle. Breaking hay bales. Clapping the heifers and stabbing the pigs with the prick of his manure-fork tines so the porkers were four-pimpled pink where he kept while he would back from his chopping the hopper.

If ever he was interrupted at breakfast, he'd swear, "goddamn, can't even eat in peace in this goddamned house!" and then flee for the barn, but not before pocketing two slices of bread for his beloved Tippy and not before also pocketing the last five cherry tarts where they broke red jam in his pocket like five little crushed birds.

The second to come to the table was the mother. She would bustle about, cleaning up the hired man's mess saying things to her own good self, such as, "That man! I was saving those tarts for the picnic. Can't he leave anything alone. I thought I'd hidden that cake. I wanted to ice it for Johnny's birthday. And so on..."

She said these things because, Tom was a breakfast glutton. He would have rummaged through the freezer down past the frost line, past the deep white burn of ruined meat seeking the deep-down treasures Irene had taken the time to hide. He'd have found and gummed down every greedy morsel. Every day he'd do the same. He'd take whatever tongue lashing was his due and like a dog prefer the punishment to the deprivation. If she baked before midnight her small hours work would be gone from the world by six a.m.. He sought and found her every hiding place and gobbled till he ached. It was a drama.

The third to arrive at table was the father. He would move through the room like a drugged bear and seat himself at the head of the harvest. The woman poured him coffee. "Cream?" "Black." Every day repeating the same echo and response. She'd set out his cereal. Grape nut flakes. Raisin Bran. Cheerios. Corn Flakes. And he would make his selection. Evaporated milk for grape nut flakes. Cow's milk cold from the refrigerator white on bottom cream on top like nylon stockings rolled once. The mother would go to the stove and scrape away at the bacon and the thin fried eggs so they came loose like filigrees of scraped away wood glue.

Then while the father dipped his lady fingers in the golden yolks, the bachelor brother came down. He always prepared his own meal. He took the ever-boiling kettle from the fire and placing his mug in a bowl he would heap in two tea spoons of instant coffee and then pour the steaming liquid until the cup overflowed and filled the bowl like a science experiment. Then he would spoon three full scoops of marmalade onto his plate and proceed to drink his hot coffee, the mug dripping and then he would eat his toast one teaspoon of jam at a time.

Of course the father and brother did not speak. The brother

might say, "Did she make bacon?" Or he might say, "Did she make porridge?" Meaning by 'she' the only woman in the room. The one named Irene. The one married to his brother. The one woman he referred to always and forever in the third person for fear that if he either engaged her directly or spoke her name aloud, all life as he knew it would end.

Next the children would emerge from their beds, the sister scratching and yawning, the son, a shambling and gangly runt in his blue-striped pajamas clutching his open fly shut. The sister ate nothing. She made a bee line for the bathroom and then took her place at the table blinking in the brilliant light like a startled nocturnal. She'd sit there mussing her hair, aping her armpits, and noshing her tongue in the slow waking of the senses that involved mostly remembering who she was, where she was, why she was there and how much she hated every minute of it. She emerged from sleep as if from a long coma or a mild anaesthetic or from amnesia suffered by a blunt blow to the head. She was a deep sleeper. And for her, sleep blent into wakefulness as oil blends with water in a slow rainbow blurring that barely mixes.

The son of the father, brother to the sister, nephew to the uncle, grandson to the old man yet to arrive pimpled his toast with home-made apricot jam and ate with his chair tipped back and yawing like a small ship in a light wind.

"Sit down in that chair!" the father would snap. "You'll break that chair! And then who'll pay for it? You?"

"Do you want to crack your skull?" the mother would say. Her sympathy revealed.

"Any spoons, mother?" the father would say, sitting half-an-arm's length from the familiar spoon drawer in the absence of spoons.

"Any salt? Any butter? Any more jam? More bacon? Bread? Coffee?" The mother moving like an obedient marionette in a tangle of strings, juggling silver, pressing the toaster like a Brailler with only one key.

The day became a recurring dream. A photograph slowly

coming clear in emulsion. Familiar ballet.

And then, after each subsequent player in the ever-repeating kitchen drama made a drab exit, after the table was cleared, the dishes were washed, stacked, dried, put away, after the floor was swept of its crumbs, and the scraps had been flung to the hogs so the swill cleared the fence like a swath of filthy light, the father-in-law limped in.

Large, long-limbed, and hungry for morning, he would not say, "Am I late? Oh you've gone an put it all away. I am sorry." No, he'd simply give his daughter-in-law a withering back of the shoulders look by lifting the lid from the porridge pot and peering in at the lamb's coat of cold woolly oat meal. He'd pluck the stuck spoon from the bacon pan and lick the white congeal. He'd break the hard left-over toast in half so it snapped in a spore of crumbs. He'd be sipping and dipping and slurping and clicking his false teeth for the seeds. He'd be unwrapping, decapping, unscrewing, slathering, spilling, and belching so his chair was surrounded in a sound of his eating and the cascading circumference of crumbs. When he was finished, he'd swallow, spit in the sink, exit the house and piss off the back porch onto the blanching petunias.

So it went, in the absence of Stella. So it went for forty years until the hired man withered up and blew away like smoke above paper. Until the father-in-law breathed his last crust. Until the sister departed and the son digressed. Until the father and mother and uncle were the last ghosts there. Pouring their coffee and spooning their jam. So Stella returns, wordless as moonshadow, saying, "Bring me the tide in a thimble. Bring me the dark in a jar."

The Essential Books for a Writer's Personal Library

1. A series of dicitonaries the most important of which would be the Oxford English Dictionary popularly referred to as the O.E.D.

2. A good Thesaurus.

3. The King James Bible

4. A good Greco-Roman mythology text and a book of the *Mythologies of the World.*

5. *Benet's Reader's Encyclopedi*a and the various Oxford Companions to Literature.

6. An encyclopedia

7. A book on proper grammar and usage

8. *A Writer's Handboo*k with the names and addresses of publishers

9. One copy each of the works of writers you have come to admire

10. The complete works of William Shakespeare

Final Words...dumb ink on a dead page...

This book cannot possibly contain everything you need to know to become the best writer you can be. Let me conclude by re-iterating the most important principles I think all writers who aspire to excellence should live by.

Write every day. Re-write everything you write. Edit for excellence. Proof read for perfection. Read anything and everything, but also read well. Read as a writer reads with a discriminating mind and a discerning eye. Be alive and alert in the world. Be interested in everything. And remember and honour your own best imaginary reader. The creator is nothing without the re-creator. The creation is otherwise dumb ink on a dead page.